A Family Way

A Family Way

by
David Barr

Wensum Books

PUBLISHED BY
WENSUM BOOKS (NORWICH) LTD
33 ORFORD PLACE, NORWICH NOR 06D
PRINTED IN ENGLAND BY
CLANPRESS, KING'S LYNN, NORFOLK
SET IN 11 POINT ENGLISH 49
PRINTED ON GLASTONBURY ANTIQUE LAID

ISBN 0 903619 17 2

CONTENTS

ILLUSTRATIONS

Foreword

In one of the later chapters of this light-hearted "autobiography" the author, a Fenland lawyer, describes how, in a busy life, his mind often goes off on flights of fancy while he lies in bed half asleep in the early morning, with the radio switched on, waiting for the 7 o'clock news.

It is in this limbo between waking and sleeping that many of his ideas seem to come to him. They are not all fanciful ideas, though by the time they get on to paper they tend to develop a whimsical flavour of their own.

Most of the material was first published in the *Eastern Daily Press* during the years 1966-1973, and a good deal of it had already been written before a biographical theme began to emerge. Here, essentially, was the story of a happy family life, beginning with a whirlwind romance in the Services (a characteristically whimsical affair); the young couple settling into their first oddly-constructed home, learning to dovetail two separate careers and an eventful home life with varying interests; family celebrations and partings, pets and hobbies; going on holiday; coping with unexpected visits from ex-girl-friends.

Through it all runs a thread of gently mocking good humour (echoed in Jacqueline Geldart's delightful illustrations) which takes the bitter taste out of life in the Swinging Seventies.

R.G.C.

Fateful Meeting

I was, 27 years and 3 months ago, serving the last weeks of my five-year sentence in the Army, in Germany, sitting periodically as an inept and juvenile judge in Westphalia. I still wake up in the night and wonder what those respectable ladies really thought who received sentences of 3 months for being in the streets after curfew.

In my spare time I filled in the hours in the despairing way of the military when a war is over, sitting in a mess and reading ancient magazines and going with others equally bored to the local club, where drinks were strong and cheap.

One evening I spotted a tall, dark American bird (as she would be called now) in the part of the bar reserved for Generals and Field Marshals and being chatted up by at least five of them. At that moment (and two men are still alive to corroborate this) I turned to my brother-in-arms and said: "That's the girl I'm going to marry." "She's not for you" he answered, thinking either of the high-ranking competition or of the large photograph by my bed of a blonde in a twin-set and pearls.

American army captains (as the bars on her shoulders indicated) were unique in the British zone, particularly ones who looked like her . . . and that halts me for a second. Were the glorious girls in our lives in those remote days really as quaint as they look in the 1940s films, with their cupid's bows in the centre of powdered faces and their compressed permanently-waved hair? The early photographs of my wife do not support this . . .

To my energetically enquiring mind, the tracing of such a vision was not all that difficult. Within a week I had not only located her mess but had achieved an ally who slept in the next bedroom. She was the doctor in charge of two vast displaced persons' camps near by — the results of the tensions in which were coming before my court almost daily. "Tell her," I said to my ally, "that her future husband will be along to see her very soon." Those engaged in the eternal chase, who really know their own minds, might note that this is a highly successful gambit.

No sooner had I passed on this piece of information than I was overwhelmed by a massive attack of chicken pox which put me into hospital for a week. During this week my nefarious matrimonial campaign was given a further spur by a letter from the twin-set and pearls telling me that we ought to think again about our joint future. She had been to the place where I had grabbed myself a job and had concluded that it was not where she wanted to spend her life. A letter like that was called, in those days, a Dear John, and they were not normally so welcome.

Out of hospital and in rude health one more, I sent a note to "her" mess telling her that I would be calling at 2 o'clock the next afternoon. I waited there for half an hour, but no one came. Then I scribbled on a piece of paper (we still have it) that I could wait no longer, that it was all off. With heavy heart I made my way to the car. At that moment an ambulance arrived in a cloud of dust and from the driver's seat, out jumped my girl.

The course of true love seldom runs smoothly. It took a whole week before we became engaged — on one day of which she retired to bed, exhausted by the mental struggle of deciding to surrender every plan she had ever made, work in China, a year in a circus, a log cabin in the Wyoming mountains. Nor did we find it easy to get married. There was a ban at the time on Anglo-American marriages, mainly designed to protect G.I.s from designing English girls who believed that their prospective husbands were oil millionaires with ranches in Texas. It needed, in the end, a dispatch rider to the most star-spangled military tycoon in the American zone to get the go-ahead.

The wedding was not quite on the scale of Westminster Abbey, but as the first inter-Allied one it was given the full treatment and backed by the whole energy of the Army. On the way to the reception (in a car belonging to one of her generals) we were stopped by a group of German women who had made a chain across the road. For an uneasy moment I wondered if some of my curfew ladies had not decided to exact a righteous revenge. Instead they festooned the car with flowers and lilac. That was the first time we learnt that we both come close to tears easily.

All those who knew us both were full of misgivings about our frenzied haste. To a man and woman they were afraid that she was making a grave mistake. So it is nice after all these years to realise that they must have been wrong, and at the same time to record an admiring tribute to someone who has pampered, spoiled, stimulated, protected, tolerated, encouraged, boosted and occasionally (at exactly the right moment) gently deflated me. I hope to be able to add more to this when our total reaches 50.

First Home

Walking with athletic gait past the almost perpetual traffic jam adjoining St. Peter's Church Gardens the other day, I saw with horror that where not long ago there had been a fine Late Georgian building with a shop in front (the very corner of the Market Place) there is now only a gaping scaffolding-strewn hole.

The fact that into the gap will, in due course, be contrived a costly and possibly tastefully built bank is no consolation to me, for what has vanished is not only a slice of the old town — but much more important, the mountainous home in which we spent the first two years of our married life. It will do no harm to the bankers if they are haunted once or twice a week by the happy echoes from that exciting piece of my past.

My wife had left me before our life together even began. She had had to return to Nebraska to free herself from the tyranny of the United States Army, to forge some sort of peace with her mother and to fetch (as she put it) her clothes. I was left with five weeks to ruminate sadly on the gloom of the lives of bachelors, and to find a resting place for us and our three pieces of furniture. With the persuasiveness of despair (and the good fortune to hear, before anyone else, of the empty house behind the shop in the Market Place) I talked the owner into letting me have the thin slice at the rear.

Thin slice it was too — with a cellar, an underground bedroom, a huge first-floor sitting room coupled to an elevated greenhouse with grapevine, a small room that was eventually converted into a kitchen, a bathroom with a great steel bath (free of any sign of paint, attached to a prehistoric geyser), and a top bedroom — all linked together by seven separate flights of stairs.

Outside there was a walled garden and another derelict greenhouse, complete with a fine crop of hay that concealed a host of ancient concrete ornaments.

It was here that we gathered together our first possessions. Multiple clusters of coupons, mystifying to both of us, enabled us to buy not only food but also furniture. From out of an Aladdin's trunk that had returned from the U.S.A. there came towels and curtains and tablecloths and bedspreads of a brightness and quality that drew sighs of envy. We bought badly painted crockery from the market, saucepans from the ironmonger's opposite (now a Co-operative shopping palace). We inherited a small dog and installed chickens in the garden greenhouse. What we failed to get hold of was more than two hundredweight of coal. Later on, this proved to be a worry, in spite of the anonymous visitor who left us a huge sack of logs at Christmas.

That winter the cold settled in in January and did not break camp until April. By early in the new year all our coal had disappeared in a series of rash blazes in the Adam fireplace. When we failed to find anyone who would ask us round for the evening, we sat cosily in the kitchen with the cooking stove switched on at all possible points. Our income was £6 a week and out of this we managed to do everything except pay the electricity bill when the day of reckoning finally came.

There are no hardships, of course, at such times and everything that I remember glitters. The discovery, for instance, that the floor in the sitting room sloped so much that when the dog misbehaved at one end, the river ran 26 feet into the greenhouse. When the thaw came, the same tilt, one storey higher in our bedroom, saved us some anguish. For three nights we lay and watched the water running along the ceiling and heard it tinkling into a variety of pans that we had scattered on the floor beyond our bed. The excitement of the first spring and summer culminated in the arrival of the new generation — dark, hairy, unspeakably ugly but, to our massive relief, with only one head.

The second winter was gayer still. By that time, we had a proper stock of fuel and some heaters. People had found out where we lived and had started coming to see us. A small increase in pay had restored the possibilities of smoking our own cigarettes and even opened up such vistas as occasional bottles of wine. Two friends had moved into four rooms a further flight of stairs above us and the traffic on the staircase doubled and redoubled.

We tried endlessly but without success to find out who had lived in the house before us. It was hard to believe that anyone had had a permanent life there in such alpine surroundings, but the cellars and the lower room were quite dark and dank enough to have sheltered a host of Victorian servants. In our time, at least, the whole building really came to life.

Then one afternoon our son, crawling in the first floor greenhouse, prised open the door that led nowhere and fell 12 feet on to the concrete slab below. He suffered no injury but suddenly the whole place turned sour on us. After going on our knees to the nearest building society we bought the first dwelling that came on to the market.

And now there will be securities where the living room was, mountains of pound notes, perhaps, where we used to have our baths. A new smiling bank manager may be sitting close to an old downstairs bedroom aching to grant what he would genially describe as Facilities. We could surely have done with some ourselves in the early times — but it is salutary to remember that being poor and being happy combined together very well.

Doctor's Husband

Many words have been written about the tribulations in the lives of doctors. Almost as many have found their way into print on the difficulties of being a doctor's wife. Few have (as far as I know) been penned on the real and significant troubles that beset the life of a doctor's husband. For the benefit of sociologists of the future, I would like to get the record straight.

The news that I was marrying a doctor — and an American one at that — had set the pulses of my whole family racing with enthusiasm. Before they even met her, each one of them (I suspect) had envisaged cosy chats (of an intimacy that their own G.P.s had so far denied them) with the new member of the family, discussing at length symptoms that were both rare and controversial. The blow fell when they discovered that to all intents and purposes my love goddess was unqualified. This cloud only vanished when a year and one pregnancy later she eventually passed the conjoint and emerged as the family's idol, with dual qualifications.

Up to that point, I had hardly suffered. We paid the examination fees and the cost of a rip-roaring correspondence course out of our gratuities. I regarded the whole thing as a promising investment, liable at any time to produce dividends in the shape of a stimulated wife and some interesting payments of money — a commodity of which we were then (and ever since have been) continuously short.

We set up a surgery in what had once been a bathroom, and a waiting room in what had once been a lean-to greenhouse. We bought a plate and hammered it into the wall. Then we waited — for about 12 hours.

The patients came in a long, steady stream, with every one of them active and demanding and in need of full-time treatment. Within a month 350 had signed on — within six months the number had grown to our agreed maximum of 500. Within another two months the number had reached 750 and the shutters were put up reluctantly, the stimulation having tended to exceed discretion.

If there is one way to fame in a country district, it is to have a reputation of absolute exclusiveness. From the moment that my wife refused to take more patients she became one of the most desirable properties in East Anglia. The situation was not relieved by a rumour that flashed round the county that she used American drugs. We both spent as much time putting people off as was spent coping with the patients. And believe me, 750 newly-acquired patients take some coping with.

It was at this stage that I declared war on the patients. They were running my wife into the ground and any moment she, not they, was going to be in need of care and protection. Worse still by far, within a space of four weeks three people said to me: "Oh, you must be Doctor Barr's Husband". Dr. Barr's husband I was and have been nearly ever since.

I could think of only one occasion on which I could reverse this situation. As the local coroner, there was always a chance that my wife might be called before me as a witness. I would have gained a tiny measure of pleasure in asking her to be seated and finding out her name and qualifications. During her 15 years in practice this situation never arose.

It was perhaps because of this psychological trauma that I and our two sons developed along spectacular lines the techniques of dealing with patients who telephoned or called at the wrong times. Icily polite, we formed a stern barrier between them and her, and our method of asking their names ("What do you say your name is?" — as though what we had heard was hardly credible), our total vagueness as to her whereabouts (when she was in the garden or washing up or out on her horse), should have been enough to diminish her list considerably; nevertheless, during her whole time in practice the pressure to join what was evidently judged to be an exclusive club never faltered.

Fortunately, my wife realised at last that to be on duty 24 hours a day for 750 patients, and to run a car, pay locums (or is it loci?) and employ help in the house to take calls while she was on her rounds was hardly economic. She retired to the comparative serenity of the local hospitals and became my wife again.

Woodnotes Wild

The lane we live in and the gardens that adjoin it have become a sanctuary for all kinds of birds. Our fruit trees are not sprayed. We kill our slugs with the greatest caution and the pines we planted, which 18 years ago were hidden by twitch, have become a dark green, sweet-smelling thicket where a hundred birds can feed without a passing cat even suspecting it. In our own garden (unlike some of the better tilled and more immaculate ones near by) we grow a fine selection of good weeds to spice the diet of the birds who would otherwise have to eke out a thinner living on our raspberries plums, calabrese (the vegetable we can spare least of all), lettuces and seedlings.

The year began well with the missel thrushes, song thrushes and blackbirds returning to their usual trees and bushes and hatching their broods with complete success. They were followed by the goldfinches and then the flycatchers, the first time we have had a family of these gay hard-working creatures yo-yoing themselves from their various hunting points. Though we had the young, our neighbours pointed out, the nest was in their garden. We had searched without reward for it in our walls and crevices and had to admit that they were probably right.

Later, and to our delight, came the flood of goldcrests, squeaking like the echoes of mice and fluttering around the branches like humming-birds, quick as shadows, agile as acrobats — yet lacking any fear of the humans whose admiring faces mooned up at them. It was hard to count their number, so quick were they and so many trees did they scour in their search for insects; there must have been at least six. I would fix them firmly in my field glasses, then when they came too close I would put on my driving glasses so as not to miss a feather or a piece of fluff.

They were not old enough to wear the golden crest and we never saw their parents — or if we did, not close enough to catch the vivid stripe. Nor did we ever hear the "cedar cedar cedar-sissa-pee" which, according to our hysterical bird book, is their song. Our neighbours told us that the parents were in their garden — where the nest was. In the back of my mind I still believe that it is hanging from one of the high branches in the pine thicket.

We made, one wakeful morning, a tape recording of the dawn chorus. In the early silence the machine picked up every note and magnified it so that the recording sounds like a liquid, lively, briskly conducted dawn orchestra. But the noises of summer are not merely confined to the birds. When the grass in the orchard is at its richest, we hear great morning sighs of contentment from our Arabian horses.

Then, with the ripening of the fruit, the tempo of the traffic in the lane quickens until one day before breakfast we look out of the window to see that the noises are coming from throngs of pickers, stimulated by the prospect of £3.50 a day, with their dogs and children, making their way to the strawberries or gooseberries. The intonations of their voices are lower, when 10 hours later they drag themselves homewards.

Even the various lawnmowers have their individual notes, the smooth well maintained one across the way, the hovercraft type one up the lane floating on its cushion of air, and the staccato, irregular spluttering of· both of ours, advertising to the world that their engines are being neglected by a pair of mechanical incompetents. The one sound, in fact, that we have not not yet heard — drowned perhaps by all the others — is the sound of the various parent birds, beaks loaded with our fur and feathers, flying from their homes in our garden to their nests in our neighbours'.

Loving Cup

Each morning we share a Loving Cup of early morning tea. Clearly the smooth and even tenor of our married life depends and thrives upon the thick sweet brew; charged and fixed with this stimulant we are both able to face more easily the rigours that follow. Few souls can see much sweetness in early morning living — but the mountainous molehills on which we would otherwise stumble, disintegrate when once the tea is coursing through our bloodstreams.

In the early years I contended with the usual difficulties that beset anyone rash enough (and lucky enough, let me quickly say) to take an American as a bride. The beloved face would often fall in the post-honeymoon days at the sight and thought of such a medicine. To her it was yet another Island perplexity, to be added to warm beer and Yorkshire pudding and bread-sauce (though not a bit more bewildering than numbing occasions I survived in America, like oyster stew on Christmas Day or the waffle, syrup and bacon combinations they give you at breakfast). Fortunately the habit formed quickly. It was not very long before the steaming morning mugful was as essential to her existence as to mine.

There are those, no doubt, who even in struggling Britain, have people knock on the door and enter, carrying tray and pot and cups and thin elegantly rolled bread and butter (permissible, this, on wet days on hard earned holidays but as a normal routine, demoralising). There are others, I know, who possess electronic apparatus that wakes them up, switches on the television, boils the water and even holds out the cup to the Patient. Both groups miss, if I may say so, the essence of the early morning tea mystique.

The basis of the whole ritual is that there must be two parties to the transaction. There must be the sufferer who crawls out of bed, stumbles blindly downstairs and creates — and to complement him (or her) there must also be the beneficiary, sleeping blissfully through the sufferer's ordeal, accepting the fruits of his labours with a delicious combination of guilt and luxury.

We are always being questioned as to who gets it most. There is no truthful answer. We both have phases of early morning energy, entirely unpredictable in their happening. Nothing is said, no advance decision made, but each day one of us will make the plunge, leaving the other luxuriating.

Creating tea in those early hours is no simple matter. Co-ordination is poor and things can go seriously wrong — like pouring the boiling water into the pot without having put the tea in. Only when pure water is added to the milk in the cup can one realise what has happened. By then the kettle will have been refilled with cold water and the whole jerky process must begin afresh.

We have both at one time or another poured the whole of a new tea packet into the pot (instead of the caddy). The resulting brew is on the strong side. There was even an occasion when I tipped a packet of sugar into the mug, with nauseating results. There are also troubles with the kettle. It always seems to me to take an absurdly long time to boil. I stare at it, then angrily tip most of its contents into the sink. Once or twice I have not left enough to fill the pot . . .

A further difficulty — and one of our own making — is our cherished collection of mugs, all pint sized and ranging from Funnies with Paw and Maw or Strychnine written on them through to Spode, Devonware and Wedgwood. We try to give them an outing in turn — with special ones for Sundays — but it is not easy to remember if the one with Troutflies or the Coronation mug has been used within the last fortnight.

Experience has shown that only we can do the job properly and produce a nicely balanced mixture at exactly the right temperature in the appropriate mug at the correct moment. Insomniac guests have occasionally clattered downstairs at about 6 o'clock and brought us lukewarm insipid doses twenty minutes later. We had to put a firm stop on guest tea-making since the morning when a vague but delicious American guest insisted on taking on the task and made it in an electric kettle. Neither we nor the kettle have been the same since.

Career Wife

They do not have an over leisurely life, going about their business and looking after us. This has just hit me sharply.

Most mornings they bring me tea in bed (though there are some on which I take it to them). Then, while I am having a relaxing bath and shave, they are busying themselves with getting breakfast and simultaneously preparing lunch and even supper. We both go off to work at the same time, but in opposite directions. They usually succeed in knocking off by a quarter to one. By the time I get back at ten past, there is the lunch on the table, steaming and succulent, everything that I dislike carefully avoided.

In the evenings they are nearly always later than I am. I have sometimes been able to have a few minutes' sleep before they return. Every now and then they wake me up after the 6 o'clock news with more tea. Sometimes there are things for me to do, but usually I cherish the hour or so until 7, a period when I can read the papers or a book and let the grit of the day slide off me.

Meanwhile, from the kitchen comes a variety of sounds, the click-clack of the ironing-board, the whirr of the washing machine, the rattle of plates and knives, forks and spoons. By seven they are ready to feed me (and anyone else needing feeding) and by seven thirty the day's eating is over. All they have to do then is get the washing-up done and make preliminary arrangements for breakfast.

Of course, that is not the whole story. Somewhere between times, beds are made, rooms are swept, tables are polished, shopping is done, dog is fed, car is filled with petrol, horse is exercised, follow-up telephone calls about their work are made. Then there is the garden. I do some, they do the rest — and that includes the vegetable patch and much of the grass. In the summer, they get out and do this before the morning tea. There is not much other time if one comes to think of it.

This catalogue of their activity is still not nearly complete. There is constant and time-consuming production of home-made wine, gallons of tomato juice are bottled in season, raspberries are frozen and turned into jam, people are coped with who come to stay, chickens are pandered to, holes in the hedge mended, committees sat on, speeches made, lectures given.

In the meantime they treat us all with enormous benevolence. It is perfectly in order for us to have an evening's fishing, or a night in London, or to be tired and pathetic at the end of the day. They are apologetic if they are away — or even late. We are allowed to make purring noises at the sight of tall dark mini-dressed creatures, but it would be clearly wrong for them to sigh at the male equivalent.

When we are ill we get ministered to in both their capacities, pampered, cosseted, heaped with books and grapes and drinks. If they were ever ill the whole machine would grind to a jerky halt. If they have ever been ill, they have never admitted it. In the evenings I say irritably, "Isn't it about time you came and sat down?" — not wanting to drink on my own. "I'll be along soon," is the usual answer, as the click-clacks, whirrs and rattles continue.

When holidays eventually come, we load the fishing rods and golf clubs and the other pleasure-producing implements and off we go, as soon as they have finished the last of the packing. When people ask them why we always go on fishing holidays they reply without malice, "He would be unbearable on any other kind of holiday — and rivers are always in lovely places."

A week ago I noticed that their replies were not quite at the normal level of friendly co-operation. "Sharp" might be one description, even downright irritable. I, feeling jaded in April had had four days with a son on the banks of the Usk, and thinking about this, there dawned inside my thick head the unshapely truth. Since our return from our fishing holiday last October there could hardly have been a single moment's break in the cooking, ironing, tidying, shopping, paying bills, working at three hospitals, hoeing, mowing, arranging, planning, thinking. Even those carefully relaxed dinner parties that I had arranged each month had merely added to a burden that was finally tending even to bend their broad shoulders.

Quietly and forcibly I telephoned a hotel in Sussex for reservations. Calmly I reported to them what I had done. No golf clubs this time, no fishing rods — just an unrefreshed career wife and her conscience-stricken husband.

No wonder she is plural.

Commuting Trials

Underneath our offices are some grizzly cellars. A rusting kitchen range indicates that people once lived a mole-like existence there, below ground level. One of these caves has been converted into a majestic strong room. In another, standing on duckboards to part them from the damp floor, is a mountain of cardboard boxes containing drafts. The code-like numbers on each one of these boxes indicate a furtive hope that its contents could be traced if the need arose. Broken panes in windows (through which people once presumably stared at the feet of passers-by) and crumbling plaster on the walls are evidence of the truth — the money has been spent upstairs; beneath us we have this ticking landmine.

Wandering through these dungeons recently, I came upon the skeleton of a large lofty bicycle, not quite a penny-farthing, but the younger son of one. It suddenly occured to me that this must have been the transport, sixty years ago, of one of the firm's early principals — used, perhaps, when the trap was being painted or the horse was lame. He had lived, I knew, in the same village as I, and the thought of the stately arrival by bicycle of Lawyer Dawbarn set me thinking.

It is not generally appreciated that one of the drawbacks of living in the country instead of a large city is that it can involve one in considerable and arduous travelling. When my speedometer clock is in good working order it registers one and nine-tenths miles from door to door — two miles each way for the purposes of any argument. It takes me six minutes if the level crossing is open, nine if it is not. I have yet to beat five minutes, even by breaking the speed limit and letting all the cylinders give their maximum performance. In spite of the distance I succeed in getting home for lunch, and to this I attribute my freedom from ulcers and the majestic and gentle flow of my stomach juices.

Not very long ago we had a fine hotel in the Ancient Borough. A long Queen Anne dining-room had been miraculously adapted to the needs of the hungry, and the food was, on the whole, delicious. It was the kind of place where men could sometimes be seen in the evenings washing down large quantities of red beef with a variety of thoughtfully tasted clarets. In times of emergency it was a good substitute for home. Change and progress have put an end to this. Where the Adam fireplace stood, a huge range has been installed and a variety of fried food and chips emerges from this all day.

The hurried but well-cooked productions of my wife (who also has a lunch-hour to observe) are much better for my health and figure. But the to-ing and fro-ing brings my daily total of six or nine minute journeys to four, to which can be added the occasional extras when I have forgotten my pen or have left a vital file behind.

But even this is not the end of the hardships of a country lawyer. Not so very long ago I was able to park, with derisive ease, outside the office, at least two days out of three. Even on the third day there was a spot to be found round the corner — where a long-dead and irascible doctor had painted "No Parking" on the road outside his house. Few people knew the secret of this mortmain ineffectiveness.

Now, with the car explosion, one looks back on that sort of easy living with nostalgia. The only way at present to find an adjacent car-space is to come to work half an hour before anyone else, and already a number of keen, observant people have joined this particular club. The choice will soon be 7.30 a.m. or the Borough Car Park. The latter has two built-in disadvantages. It is quite a quarter of a mile away from the office (more productivity being lavishly frittered away, off-setting the benefits to the waistline) and it is situated in a tarmacadam jungle of lime trees. The morning's shiny car is covered with a scurf of lime-droppings by lunch-time, a formidable deterrent to one who likes a car to look elegant but has an unshakable aversion to washing it.

It looks as though it is going to be 7.30 a.m. in future, but it is not going to be an easy target to achieve. In the black moments of the winter, an hour should be time enough to get washed, shaved and breakfasted, but 6.30 on a February morning has never shown promise of becoming one of my favourite moments. In the summer it will be worse. There is wheat to be given to the chickens, potatoes must be dug, raspberries picked, beans and peas harvested. Getting-up time could become as early as six. For one whose stamina is by no means world class, it is going to be a long day.

Does anyone, by any chance, know a craftsman who can restore to mint condition a large, heavy, stately 60-year-old bicycle?

Poop, Poop

I fell in love with what I will call The Animal after carelessly picking up a brochure in a garage. Would that I had never done so! I was lost from the moment I saw those sleek enchanting lines as it stood outside a mansion, poised to receive a breath-taking girl who tripped down the steps towards it, carrying her jet-set luggage. I had completely abandoned hope as I devoured the rich leather seats, gloated over the maze of machinery under the bonnet — and absorbed the onomatopoeic description of the whispering thrum-thrum of all those horses.

The price seemed appalling — but not so appalling that if I forgot all the costly extras, it might not be just within reach, with a good sale of my own car and the eager helping hand of my kindly bank manager. Dry mouthed and furtive (I had not confessed to my family this hot, impetuous decision. I knew there would be a Whatever-do-you-want-one-like-that-for; you-never-go-over-60 reaction) I entered the marble hall and, surrounded by gleaming but lesser models, spoke to the Manager. This was surely the kind of business that he rarely had the opportunity of doing. "Going to make a change," I said, keeping the best for last. "My own car, of course, is very good. A great buy for anyone — 60,000 miles and not a hint of trouble . . ."

"Good," said the Manager, smiling encouragingly.

"So I've decided" (it all came out in a rush) "to step up a little and have an Animal." To my surprise, the Manager's smile seemed to have become a little fixed — I hurried on.

"I'll have a white one, I think, with the red upholstery, The hard top's cheaper — and I certainly wouldn't need overdrive with all those cylinders — nor power steering — just the basic job." The Manager lifted his hand. "Slow down," he said, "these Animals are like gold-dust. I've only had one in 18 months." "Put me on the list," I answered brashly. I knew about motor-dealers' built-in pessimism. I would certainly not be the one to be surprised when the 'phone rang and the triumphant voice said "I've got you your Animal."

Meanwhile, I studied the second-hand-car advertisements. They were encouraging. My year, my model, was for sale at £800. Giving £50 for pulling it together and putting a shine on it and taking off another £50 for profit, I was still left sitting prettily in the £700 range. With the help I have referred to and by realising some Unit Trusts (still below the price I gave for them three years ago) I was home and dry.

I began to visualise the day I pulled in, at home, in the powerful gleaming white dream. I told my friends that I had decided — just this once — to go mad. "I'm getting an Animal." They gasped. "You're going to be worth knowing," said the nubile ones (was that what I had in mind all the time?). "Good for you," said my contemporaries, thinking that they might need, one day, my support for a similar venture. "Have you reached your second childhood?" asked my family, seeing their inheritance vanishing. But I could take it all, my mind in a whirl of modest acceleration and unostentatious bravura. "Poop, poop," said my wife, mind fixed on "The Wind in the Willows."

Then one day the telephone rang and it wasn't the police or a wrong number, or an invitation to a wine and cheese orgy. "We've found an Animal for you — when would you like to try it?" Though the receiver trembled my voice was steady. "See you in an hour's time," I replied without hesitation.

There was already a small crowd round it as I walked out, like a Grand Prix driver off on a lap. Almost coyly I took my place beside the Manager. "You drive it off," I said, embarrassed at finding myself the cynosure of all eyes. It was charcoal grey with brown interior. Later we changed seats and lovingly I crunched the gear lever. The engines noise was like the muffled thrum-

thrum of an ocean liner. I caressed the accelerator, not daring to plunge it lower. The back of the seat squeezed my kidneys.

"Poop, poop," I thought to myself, dazedly watching the wet kerbs cream by. "Press the overdrive switch," said the Manager. "Listen to the swish of the power-steering," said the Manager. "What do you think of the special inter-changeable top — hard and soft?" . . . "Tell me, very quietly," I asked in a small voice, "what this thing costs."

There was a pause, a slightly embarrassed pause. Then he told me. With the additions, it was £200 more than my worst fear. "And heaven knows," he added, "when we'll see another."

"My own car," I continued with courage, though I knew the tide was running out, "what'll we make on that?" The Manager's voice became sepulchral. "We've got to face it — the second-hand market's terrible just now — glutted — and yours isn't good. It's rough. I doubt if we could sell it — but I'll not beat about the bush. We'll give you £500 and take the consequences."

So now I'm buying a normal car, one of a kind there are plenty of and which, therefore, are not much wanted. They seem delighted to give me £650 for my rough old job.

So the inheritance remains intact, and by the time the new one is worn out, I'll be far too ancient to dream of any more Animals.

Ex-Girl Friends

Apart from my understanding wife, my family consists of two strong sons, a 17-year-old Arabian horse, a beautiful honey blonde Labrador, some chickens and ducks and half a dozen or so ex-girl friends. That my beautiful friendships with the latter have continued so long is due, I think, to the fact that I must have been almost incredibly unattractive in my late teens and early twenties.

I was lucky to be young at a golden time (and it was not so very long ago, it should quickly be added, despite the morning cough, the breathlessness, the thinning hair and a disinclination to launch myself into swimming pools unless the water temperature is 70 degrees or more). In those days, hardly gone, it was possible to lead a bright, full life on the pound a week left over after paying for digs; my eligibility was markedly increased by a £100 legacy which financed a very cosy car indeed. By taking a few thrifty steps, like free-wheeling downhill and parking on a slope so that first gear was never engaged, I found it possible to run the car during the summer months and even buy the girl friends a beer or two or a 1s.6d. seat in the cinema at the end of the journey.

There were many, of course, at the time who were not so affluent as I and it was this financial advantage, I think, that gave me (before the Army swallowed me up and left the corridors of courtship bare) as attractive a series of girl friends as any bachelor could wish for. Rambling through the lavender-scented drama-packed pages of a 5-year diary recently, I was able to evoke the excitements and setbacks of those years. But two things struck me with vigour. One was the splendid array of Joans, Rachels, Charmians, Anns, Serenas and Patricias with whom I spent so much time. The other was the complete and total lack of romantic success that attended each liaison. I think, however, that it was this absence of emotional commitment, on their part at least, that kept the friendships intact; there was no sudden end because, alas, nothing much had ever begun.

The first one that came back into my life was a tall dark girl who had once been terrifyingly attractive. She was so sought after that to take her out was an event in itself. She was so sought after that she was, in fact, pretty arrogant — but I was a convenient unattached male and was allowed to bask in her exotic presence quite frequently. She was the sort of girl one talked about to one's friends and said "It would be hell to be married to her, but worth it". I used to have a drink before meeting her, to bolster up my courage. One night when I had not been married long the telephone rang and that well-remembered voice tinkled at the other end. She was stranded in Peterborough after a train journey from Scotland. Could I rescue her? The next morning I heard downstairs an earnest and male-excluding conversation and later divined that my wife was bottling up some important piece of news. After she had gone I learnt the desperate story. Somewhere — on the train perhaps — she had accumulated some very undesirable creatures in her hair — and they had last been located on our guest room pillow. This unhappy incident has formed the basis for a lasting friendship beween her and my wife.

Almost the first girl I fell desperately in love with (when I was 17) was some six years older than I and so beautiful that she was said at the time to be an improvement on Ginger Rogers, the current love-goddess. She was a star turn at the Croydon Repertory Theatre, but managed to blend with her charm an almost unbelievable vagueness. When we had dates the odds were long against her turning up at the right time or place. She left her belongings scattered round the country. When she bothered to use make-up it hardly ever reached the right spot. At 23 it was wholly delightful. On our way north one day we decided to call at the school where she lived with her husband-headmaster. She had become a charming rotund mother of five. The only way in which I could have recognised her was from her lipstick — which was carefully pencilled in about an inch and a half below her lower lip. We see quite a bit of her and her family and they, too, use us as a staging post on their way south.

My biggest moment of all before marriage was a strapping 5 ft. 10 in. Junoesque blonde called Catriona; I had made record progress with her by reaching for a short period the stage of being "unofficially engaged", a state that gives some of the drama of the real thing without any of its commitments. She married early and has been marrying ever since. Between husbands she comes and stays with us and brings us up to date on the dolce vita. Unfortunately one of her pet themes is her bewilderment that my wife should ever have married someone like me.

Other ex-es are, I am glad to say, continually dropping in and providing our life with infinite variety, but none quite so dramatically as an American girl friend whom I and a friend competed entirely unsuccessfully for some years back. We used to meet and discuss ruefully our lack of progress and neither of us were surprised when she married an Oil Magnate. Contact dropped to the occasional Christmas card stage when one day this summer the telephone rang. There was no mistaking that slinky Baltimore accent. She asked us to eat with her at the Hilton. We couldn't make it. She said she had just divorced her husband and was taking a short vacation. We made sympathetic noises on the two telephones. It was then that she asked for the address of her other former boy friend; I have been kidding myself ever since that she was making a sentimental journey. One good thing has emerged from this non-meeting. My son on his way home from the U.S.A. will be staying with her and meeting three of her five gorgeous daughters. I like to feel that there's some continuity in these things.

Can I Help You?

As a thoroughly liberated man, I am screened from many of life's baser occupations — such as shopping — by a wife who is warmly determined to keep high my middle-aged morale. The shameful truth is that once inside a shop I undergo a very unpleasant character change. I turn, as if by magic, into a strange blend of prima donna and mouse.

The prima donna element causes me to expect instant, grovelling and obsequious service, including such things as all other customers being pushed unceremoniously aside, the immediate presence of the managing director or, at the very least, the general manager and — most important of all — the unhesitating production of exactly what I have come to buy.

Happily not a sign of any of these pent-up hopes can be seen on my still and placid face. Very much to the contrary, my demeanour appears to be so humble and my personality appears to be so grey that the customers push me unceremoniously aside and I find it impossible, even after the loudest clearings of the throat and "Excuse me, sirs" (addressed to the tycoon behind the counter), to attract anyone's attention. At this point I normally stage an unnoticed demonstration by striding pointedly out of the shop — knowing only too well that exactly the same thing will happen when I enter the rival boutique across the street.

All shops frighten me, but none so much as clothing shops, particularly men's clothing shops, with their military-moustached dummies, their riding crops in the window and the general impression that every customer spends his life between grouse moor and cocktail party.

There are times, of course, when the place is empty and after the boys and girls have discussed to the full their plans and ambitions for the coming evening, someone will approach me and ask, sharply, "Yes?" It is then that the mouse in me comes squeaking to the fore. Commercially speaking, I am already lost.

"I would like to buy a shirt," I say, "size 16."

"Do you want an Acrivel or an Orlander?" asks the draconian salesman, tipping my end of the see-saw to the ground with a thump.

"Er, something easy to wash," I stutter, "and pinkish" — making sure that there can be no misunderstanding. I do not really know what I do want, but there is always the hope — one that quickly dwindles — that there will be put before me something that I have been waiting for all my life, which I can quickly pay for and be gone with. All this time the salesman has been putting himself into an unassailable position by pulling shirt after unbelievable shirt from drawers, shelves, counters and window displays. In the end, to save face, I buy three that I can never wear and bolt from the boutique feeling that the price of freedom and release was comparatively small.

Acquiring a suit has now become such an ordeal that on the last occasion, having leafed my way through a dozen pattern-bundles, I let the expert choose for me — thereby ridding himself of a cloth that he must have believed himself stuck with for the rest of his career — and providing me with clothing in chocolate green and straw mottling that I have yet to find the moment for wearing. In the back of my mind I am thinking of a début at a Cup Final (if I can get a ticket) because the colours would guarantee complete neutrality and freedom from assault by either faction.

Strangely, a recent survey has revealed that shopping is something that many people do for pleasure — an occupation as exciting to the participants as fishing or playing golf or any of the more congenial pastimes. Furthermore, it is claimed shopping is a cheap hobby because if properly played it rarely creates any need to spend money. The Wembley of shoppers is a day in a big city with innumerable coffees and snacks interspersed by idyllic relaxed wanderings among the stores, pulling out, feeling, caressing, examining, testing and pricing articles of every kind and establishing a wholesome and enviable ascendancy over the sales staff.

Even Friday evening shopping in the supermarket can be made, it appears, an exhilarating and cost-free family experience. Half those unfortunate shoppers who find the prison gates yawning before them after being discovered with assorted unwanted and unpaid-for objects in their bags, may be innocents whose dreamy journeys through the rows of goodies have led them into absent-mindedness — though this would not be a defence that many lawyers would feel might be successful.

A stern distinction must be made between the purely feminine hobby of shopping and the more everyday task of going, list in hand, to buy something from a shop. The five-day week has opened up unending dangers for the unwary and unliberated husband as he sets forth for the town on a Saturday with the little woman, wondering if he is likely to be at the George at midday. If he is not careful he will find himself looking like Father Christmas under a load of parcels few of which will turn out to bear any relation to what his list ordered him to acquire.

The words of John Philpot Curran are worth remembering: "The condition upon which God hath given liberty to man is eternal vigilance; which condition if he break, servitude is at once the consequence of his crime, and the punishment of his guilt."

Mighty Stetson

Some people do not wear hats — or if they do, only on rare occasions. Others keep a hat always at hand and wear it if they ride in a car or go shopping or, even, dig in the garden. We are non-wearers. I do not own a single one, and my wife's hats have been rarer than leap years. Without the benefit of personal experience I suspect that the treasures kept by a hat-wearing wife must be troublesome. It would be difficult to isolate a single one, surely, out of a store of several hundred (one, perhaps, for each weekday of the year) stacked in layers and heaps, filling wardrobe, cupboard and attic. The only three major hats my wife has possessed during our bright and lovely years together have acquired names and reputations and have become surrounded by small legends.

Her first hat (I remember it vividly) was a little straw pill-box, too small, as it turned out, for its final duty. It perched on the back of her head, St. Trinian-wise, held there by a ribbon or a band. We bought it for a funeral, but it came into its own at a wedding then achieved a modest immortality at the christening of our eldest son. There we all sit, people forgotten, dead, hated, or still loved, in our absurd dated clothes and hair styles, looking pale and solemn as everyone does in twenty-year-old photographs (as though the doors had shut too early on the queue for the dole) and with the straw pill-box giving the sole touch of gaiety. It had a sad end, a year or two later, left under the seat of an old-fashioned propeller plane after a child had been sick into it.

Phyllis was the next hat, a constant companion at various great occasions, called after a tame pigeon which it closely resembled. After eight years or so people would enquire politely about Phyllis (the hat) and greet its appearances with pleasure.

Then one day we were unwise enough to wash Phyllis (the pigeon) in detergent and next morning found her shocked but snow-white corpse on the lawn. To have worn Phyllis (the hat) again would have seemed indecent.

And then came the mighty Stetson, the most triumphant of all successes, wide-brimmed and of finest felt with a red satin lining and a leather thong round the crown, coming from Wyoming and costing more than an acre of prairie. Looking like a rodeo queen or one of the dark Spanish ladies in sherry advertisements, my wife for three whole months led the nation's most fashion-conscious hat-wearers. It was only when Princess Anne followed that the avalanche came. Even so, until the crisis, the Stetson enriched every occasion.

The crisis involved an important wedding and the purchase of what she called her "mother-in-law's suit". Painstakingly this was gathered together, garment by garment, shoe by glossy shoe, a delicious cocktail of youth and maturity, swing and square, way-in and way-out. "And," she said, "the hat's the best ever."

The night before the wedding was staged a dress rehearsal and mother-in-law appeared in all her finery — displaying for the first time the hat that was to be the fairy at the peak of the Christmas tree, the candle on the top of the cake. Not a word was said by any of us, but we all knew, she too, that the mauve and tomato coloured combination of tea cosy and turban was totally and hopelessly wrong, a confidence trick played by an over-zealous hatter.

There was no more shopping time and only one course left. Out came the stiff brush, the wet sponge and the iron and in half an hour the dress rehearsal was in full swing again. On the day, it was unanimously agreed that no hat looked gayer, more serene and more eye-catching than her noble if time-worn Stetson.

Family Neckwear

In our bedroom are two cupboards, built into the walls, that contain our total raiment — His on the left. Hers on the right. Stretched across the inside of my door is a strong plastic wire. Draped over this is the family's supply of ties. We call it the "Tie Bank" or in gayer mood, the "Tiecotheque". With the door shut, our room presents a sober, restrained and appropriately dignified appearance — but open the door and it is like a peep into a dazzling hothouse. Several square feet of blazing colour illuminates the whole scene.

Most of the ties — the contributions of the Bank's other customers — are the good, straightforward products of some excited Carnaby Street muse. The duller, more sober ones — my own — are more interesting, linked as many of them are to spicy or frightening or emotional episodes in my past.

Take for instance the dark blue silk one with lions on it. It was given to me by a friend who said she had found it under her bed one morning. The last time I wore it was in a crowded bar. An enormous man came up to me, clapped me on the back and said: "It's great to see one of our first team players". He then mentioned the name of a world-famous Rugby club. It took me five minutes' hard talking to prove that, though similar, it was in fact the tie of a very insignificant golf club, all of whose members were entitled to wear it.

Next door to that now forbidden tie is a dark red silk one. A well-known London Club? A businessmen's lunch and talk group? Not a bit of it — Wisbech Town Football Club, a memory from the days when we were proud to wear it. Once at a petrol station at Peebles it provoked a long friendly conversation with the attendant, who called me Jock and asked about next

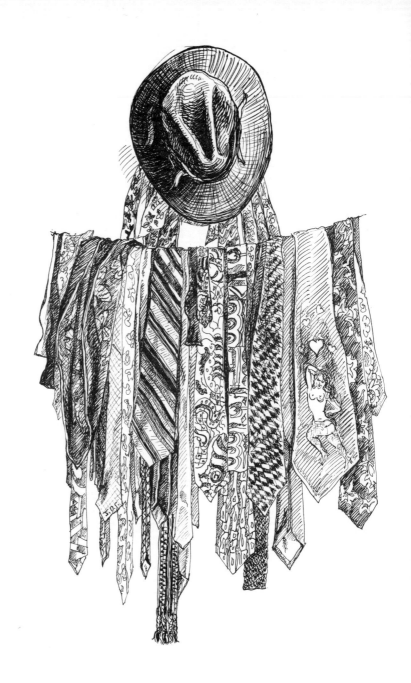

season's prospects. I have been trying ever since to discover a Scottish F.C. with the initials W.T.

Not so drab is a crimson one with white spots that I bought in a rash moment in an attempt to throw off the after effects of 'flu. It caught the eye and fancy of a delicious blonde, who before the party was over had snipped a bit off its end. The whole story sounded unlikely when I explained it to my wife.

Then there is the dark striped one I bought on an impulse for £2.50 one day in London. It is specially designed for those who suffered at the same school as I did, to wear in London. I have never dared to put it on, in case I am recognised after all these years as the Sneak of the School House, and the nasty little boy who avoided the O.T.C.

The regimental tie is worth a mention, too. Its vivid colours make it unmistakable at thirty yards. It got me involved one evening in one of those appalling sessions with two other wearers in which we endlessly and gloomily discussed the delights of the good old days.

Apart from a couple of sad many-times-ironed black bow ties for use when there is no way of avoiding wearing a dinner jacket, these are all that are left to me. The bunch of puces and indigos and browns that I had thought so thoroughly crisp were taken to a jumble sale. After being priced at 6d. each with no takers, they were finally sold for seven for 6d., or fifteen for 1s. If I knew a Latin phrase that denoted that glory is short-lived, I would use it.

One of the conditions of our banking system is that each customer shall make periodical additions to the Bank's assets. One morning recently I was accordingly goaded into making six purchases as my own special contribution. Not daring to brave the derision that would follow my buying ties of the sort I usually wear, I bought what I hoped would be six compromises.

The most sombre of these — a light-headed thin piece covered with a selection of cherries, grapes and chrysanthemums — I wore the next day. The effect was demoralising. Wherever I went

I was met with groans and gasps. Complete strangers winced, acquaintances were sarcastic, friends made remarks about second childhood. It has become increasingly clear to me that the Island Race will fail to see a new beard or a crimson waistcoat or a daringly designed tweed, but a tie is a magnet that draws every eye. At my age, I have realised, membership of a Tie Bank carries few advantages.

If one is really anxious to introduce a dash of colour to the drab everyday working uniform, it is still possible, without fear or insult, to get away with socks of greater than usual vividness. A flash of emerald or the nearest hint of crimson between well-polished shoe and sober trouser leg gives no one any excuse for ribaldry. For this reason for many years I have owned a few pairs of expensive, highly-patterned socks. Searching for them this morning I was enraged to find that the drawer contained none but the stock heathers, sparrows and straws. Finally, after a tense search, they were tracked down to a big drawer in the bedroom of one of the Tie Bank's other customers. Among a number of good-looking pairs, mine were still outstanding. I was informed, courteously, that it had been decided to start a Sock Bank.

It'll be money next.

Nights of Wassailing

Every summer, each Wednesday evening, I enter the chaste, secret world of Mine Host, serving behind the magic half-circle of the bar at a small local club. One of these days, I hope, one of those beaming photographs will be taken of myself and my senior barman, smiles wide, polishing-cloths in hand, captioned "Geoff and Dave are here to serve you from 8 to 10 each Wednesday."

Our bar is a small cog in the intricate finances of the Riding Club. Our duties are two fold — to serve the thirsty members and their friends, and to accumulate during the summer a handsome profit to swell the Club's funds.

Work for the junior barman begins early when he sets to with brush and dust-pan clearing up the mess he failed to clear up the previous Wednesday. Floor swept, it is then his job to turn to the bar itself. Acid experience has taught the lesson that it makes life difficult if the glasses are not rinsed out on the night they are used. Week-old beer stains become difficult to remove.

The glasses, therefore, are customarily rinsed (in cold water, unfortunately — the electrician has still not been to deal with the heater) and laid on the draining-board. A week later they are dry and can be placed on the shelves behind the bar — ready for use, if not exactly gleaming. A rough sweep of the floor behind the bar (which the customers cannot see), a quick wipe of the Formica surface, and all systems are go.

The arrival of Geoff at about 7 o'clock is the evening's next important moment. No judge ever arrived in court, no Chancellor took his seat on the Woolsack with more solemnity. A quick check to see that we have change and have remembered to order some beer — and Geoff and Dave are ready for action.

We barmen have to learn the tricks of the trade, and we have picked them up, over the years, the hard way. It might be appropriate to say here that the tricks of the trade that amateur barmen at our sort of club bar practise are very different from those known to the professionals who are, I am sure, bound by an entirely different set of ethics.

It took us quite a long time, for instance, to find our way round the opened bottle problem. We both went through a phase of opening bottles of Brown when Light was ordered — and vice versa — leaving us with an opened bottle for which, at the moment, there was no home. Pluckily we used to pay for and drink these ourselves. Now we bang the cap on again, and when that evening — or even next week — we get the right order — we whip the opened one out of the crate, go through energetic motions with the bottle-opener, and serve. No one has ever complained.

We have also had difficulties with the profit margin on draught beer. If all goes exactly to plan and not a drop goes astray there is only £2.50 to be won on each barrel. Drops with us have a strong tendency to go astray. We have awful times uniting the new barrel to the gas cylinder — the quantity that sometimes squirts across the bar must run into quarts.

We get diverted, too, by the more attractive of our customers. Before we know it the stuff is gushing on to the floor. Now we have a universal system (that works wonders) of not quite filling every glass.

It is particularly easy with shandies — there is so much fizz that a glass that seems to be brimming over is always well short of the half-pint measure.

Our real handicap is our lack of customers. Ours come in ones and twos. A ten shilling round draws appreciative gasps from both of us. Our average evening's takings come to less than £5, of which we normally contribute £2. We do not drink the profits — we make them. Even so our barman-customer relationship is a very happy one — we treat everyone with equal courtesy, whether he is a double Scotch, a Coco Cola or a mere half-pint of still orange. By now we know their habits so well that we don't ask "The usual?" We have it poured and ready to drink by the time the customer has reached the bar.

Every now and then, of course, strangers arrive and our hopes rise that our fondest dream will come true. One night, we hope, some man, rich beyond mortal ken, will walk in and order doubles for everyone in the bar, six pounds worth perhaps in one wonderful order. We eye every newcomer with this delightful possibility in mind — but so far the miracle has not happened. Even so, takings this year are up. With any luck we shall beat last summer's profit of £17.61p.

When They're Away

On the rare occasions when our family can introduce a note of reproach into their relationship with the mainstay of their lives — fishing tackle tidied away, favourite shirts taken to be washed after only one day's use, that sort of setback — it gives a sharp impression that we are just helpless people overshadowed by immense power in the background.

"They", I must quickly add, are very good to us. They provide for us in a way we hardly deserve. They rarely leave us, even for a day. This clearly explains the confusion that arises when they do. We have grown into cosseted creatures, unable to cope with the hardships of living without them. We miss them badly when they go — as they did recently, to a three-day medical conference.

It is hard to understand why, when abandoned in this way, we behave as we do. Perhaps it is because if we thrived too vigorously and housekept too successfully there might be a danger of other conferences, other absences. There is no necessity for the hardships we suffer. Choice meats are, no doubt, if we would only look, available in the refrigerator. The anonymous bundles that lie there uninspected contain, for sure, delicious beef or cold chicken or rashers of bacon. There are cupboards in the kitchen in which are stacked, for sure, countless tins of soup and sardines and stewed steak. We know only too well where the potatoes are, and for any eye to see there are cabbages and onions and cauliflowers in the garden.

Neither are we hopelessly incompetent. We are well aware that saucepans can be filled with water, water boiled, food simmered and cooked. It could be no impossibility for us to contrive properly cooked meals for ourselves on graciously laid tables. Yet when they have left us, a grey lethargy descends and, almost masochistically, our standards are allowed to sink to Stone Age depths.

To wash up, we tacitly decide, is invidious enough. To wash up more than necessary is absurd. So saucepans must not be dirtied, cups used for tea must be used again for coffee, saucers must remain on their shelves. The trinity of knife, fork and spoon can be ignored; a spoon alone determinedly used in conjunction with dextrous fingers will do the work of the three. A new use is soon found for the Formica top of the kitchen table. It is, if one gives it some steady thought, very much like a vast plate. So we eat off it — rinsing away the remains of our meal with a few cleansing strokes from a damp cloth.

So far as food is concerned, we live on capital. We make no efforts to go and buy the things we would more greatly enjoy. Shopping is no more attractive than washing-up. We wade grimly through the packets of cereals — finishing even the two highly coloured boxes, the chaff-like contents of which had remained uneaten for months. Milk, of course, is in good supply while existing arrangements continue, and we have brought into use a 7 lb. tin of sugar, which is kept available at all times on the useful kitchen table. Tea is well within our capabilities and we discover, at an early stage, that hot water added to the pot in which our morning tea was brewed (we could not survive without that) makes quite a fair warm brown drink at breakfast. We cut down, in this way, the difficulties that arise when tea leaves are poured into the sink.

Bread, too, appears daily on the kitchen window-sill, and we devour this eagerly with the remaining butter and marmalade — breaking it into hunks rather than cutting it. This easy living is coupled strenuously with invitations to all main meals being begged by us, softening the kind hearts of our friends with piteous stories of our hardships, battening on their generosity like leeches. All our weights were maintained during their absence.

Meanwhile mildew settled gently upon the rest of the house. The flowers died in their vases. We climbed into beds untouched since morning. The floors became covered with the daily papers. Cushions remained crumpled, cupboard doors open, drawers pulled half out. Cups, mugs and glasses lurked in unexpected places. The ash-trays looked like a series of Stop Smoking advertisements.

And then, one evening, in a flash, the chaos disappeared. Vacuum cleaners emerged from retirement, brooms bristled, flowers were picked and turned into arrangements that would have graced a Floral Festival. When within 15 minutes after the completion of Operation Spring Clean we heard the sound of her tyres on the gravel, the establishment was spick enough to receive the Queen.

Greetings over, she said, "It's lovely to be home: the place I stayed at was filthy."

All the same, I'm glad they don't put us to the test too often.

Living Without TV

We have not got it and we have never had it. After all this time I don't think that we ever will. Believe me, I admit this with no feeling of pride. We have put ourselves, by our neglect, not only beyond the pale, but into an entrenched position from which it is impossible to retreat. The whole situation has slyly crawled up on us and turned itself into a matter of principle. We have become all too like the politicians who state publicly and categorically eighteen times that they are dead against something and then find it expedient to be for it. On second thoughts, our problem would not trouble many politicians at all.

The most frenzied Anti in the family is my priceless wife. For one reason and another she hates television with venom and determination. In the days when she could be persuaded to give it a glance, the screens would dissolve into the kaleidoscopic mutations of circles and lines — like the last shuddering patterns before an anaesthetic brings unconsciousness.

Now, when the view is so much clearer, the prejudice remains, though it is not only the quality of the picture that makes her quiver. Our children emerged into adulthood unscathed by its effects. So powerful is the parental influence that they too have built-in prejudices. Certainly they have no Freudian longing to sneak off and drown themselves in the clandestine pleasures of the small blue screen.

As for myself, I realise with dreadful clarity that one of the nation's major addicts has been lost in me. I am well aware that I would have been fully capable of glaring at it unceasingly, night in, night out, complaining bitterly, but carefully ignoring the remedy that the adjacent switch would always hold out to me.

At one point my wife (sensing danger) declared firmly that the moment a set had been installed, she would go home, with vigour, to her mother. It was only when, a year later, we had bridged the gap of 6,000 miles that parted them and discovered three sets in the old homestead — two black and white and one coloured — that she realised that her threat was an empty one.

The absence of a box is a burden that needs tact, character and courage to sustain. People who have it resent, in some explained way, this idiosyncrasy — or at least react to it very strangely. However tactfully and humbly the confession is made, the ardent viewers regard it as insult. We are instantly accused of being either snobs or inverted snobs.

Others less ardent tend to launch into pitiful, intimate and embarrassing apologies. "The children needed it" they say, or "We never have the thing on ourselves" or "Of course, we only turn it on for concerts and the news". We begin to feel like Red Guards, faced by a group of revisionist swine. Curiously enough, the same people, if fortunate enough to own a well-stocked deep-freeze, would never allow themselves to notice our failure to possess one of these.

The kindly men who sell electrical appliances are difficult too. Each one thinks that his competitor has managed to sell us a four hundred volt, quadruple-tubed, super heterodyne receiver with a six square-foot screen and they all regard us with ill-concealed disappointment.

The absence of television cuts us off, without any doubt, from the mainstream of a number of topics of conversation. The identity of a whole race of famous men and women is concealed from us. When we hear how superb old so-and-so had been last night, we have learned to look tactfully agreeable, despite the fact that the name of old so-and-so means no more to any of us than one picked with a pin from a telephone directory.

Moreover, apart from the people, there are whole situations of which we have no knowledge, countless creations of which we know nothing. I was once one of the judges of a display of decorated floats and helped to award the first prize to some strangely and ingeniously dressed people who called themselves "The Glogs" or "The Plops" or something of the sort. It was weeks before I accidentally learned that they were characters in a TV serial.

We, the television-less, have our compensations. We know all there is to know about sound radio, from John Dunne, through The World at One, to the Sunday evening programmes featuring the voices of Messrs. Wilson and Heath. Furthermore, we have recently acquired a radiogram which does everything but trot round the room, and which picks up the BBC at Norwich, farm news and all, and Force 10 without effort. Moreover, it needs a small aerial, and I keep hoping that the piece of H-shaped machinery that is now attached to our chimney will put a few minds at rest.

And in moments of emergency we have neighbours who are good-looking, kind, generous and the possessors of an enormous set with a screen several feet long. It is to them that we creep when the World Cup is on or the 2.45 at Lingfield looks extra promising. But even now, when my wife can be persuaded to come along, a sly look in her direction will detect her sitting there bravely, eyes glazed and angled firmly ten degrees to the right of the crystal clear picture, thinking quiet thoughts about the days when they didn't have it in America either.

Pursuit of Culture

As a family we are painfully short on Culture. One of us, it is true, can play "Stranger on the Shore" on clarinet — but as a Mozart man, he is a non-starter. Another survived on one desperate occasion a twenty-minute struggle accompanying some carol singers on the piano. We go to hear the London Philharmonic when it plays in the area, or make honest plans to. Very occasionally we attend a pre-London play in Cambridge. Otherwise our contact with art and intellect is shamefully scanty.

True we have no television, but we haunt other people's rabidly when there's something good on, like boxing or Match of the Day. Family conversation hardly, if ever, touches on Sartre, Eliot or Benjamin Britten. Monica English's paintings are far more likely to enthuse us than Rodin's sculpture. Faced with the choice of "The Sound of Music" or something by Jean Cocteau, we would plump for Julie Andrews. Our brows are somewhere beneath our chins.

It was therefore a little surprising when we decided to book tickets for an Albert Hall concert and with no further delay sent the necessary cheque. We did this with our eyes wide open — knowing the difficulties that would face us. It is clearly easier to be less uncouth if one lives in Kensington or Paddington. A mountain of difficulties lies between those who live in the country and a 7.30 p.m. London concert. It means, for instance, leaving home in the middle of the afternoon and not getting back till one in the morning. There is never a moment for feeding and the sound of music is too often spoiled by the uneasy rumblings of our stomachs.

At any time, moreover, between the arrival of the tickets and the night, I am likely to start totting up the total of four railway-fares, snacks, programmes, taxis, and to suggest immediate cancellation and writing off the cost of the tickets, as a desperate economy measure. As an insurance against this, I let drop news of our enterprise to numbers of impressionable friends. After that, one is committed. The main steel in my resolution springs from my enjoyment of the ever rarer occasions when we go out as a family. We are a close-knit, deadly little team with a host of esoteric private amusements that must be intensely annoying to the heavily exluded outsiders.

This particular adventure had more than its fair share of crises. Two days beforehand the youngest one of us retired to bed with 'flu and a glowing temperature. My wife immediately announced her determination not to abandon her ailing chick. The ailing chick, near normal by the day, finally persuaded her to abandon him and at the last moment we located my god-daughter to come in his place. Her long blonde hair and mini-skirt constituted (as I saw it) no noticeable drawback to the occasion.

It is at the moment when we finally take our seats in far-flung auditoria like the Albert Hall that I say to myself for the first time, "I'm glad we came". After the Empire and the Hippodrome these places are big. Compared to the 350 one might expect in the Great Hall of the College of Further Education, there is a stimulating excitement in being surrounded by several thousand like-minded people. It is we, after all, who create the atmosphere that sparks the artists to their greatest efforts. With the arc-lights needling the stage and the background noises of a hushed packed crowd, we realise that we are contributing to an occasion of consequence.

The crowd on this particular night was more than usually attractive. The middle-aged were there, a middle-aged élite, I thought — and significantly many of the older men were

escorting young and attractive girls, their daughters no doubt
— or god-daughters. Mainly, though, it was a young audience,
beardless and well-dressed, not a chip visible on any shoulder.
It was not the sort of occasion, of course, to attract anything
but the best.

Finally, the lights dimmed, figures appeared on the dark
stage, a regiment of spot-lights ignited and the evening's
entertainment had begun. We sat back and soaked ourselves in
the sunlit rhythms of Herb Alpert and his Tijuana Brass.

Family of Weepers

As an inveterate and unashamed weeper, I would like to launch here and now, please, a campaign for Kindness to Those That Cry. Not sympathy — that would make it worse.

The British universally condemn crying as cissy, unmanly and degenerate. And a very good thing too, I can hear someone gruffly say. We are allowed to shed a limited number of well-concealed tears at funerals, and there are one or two of the greater Royal occasions at which a lump in the throat and some energetic swallowing can be got away with. Apart from these occasions (and when a keen east wind is blowing) tears are absolutely out.

"Crybaby" is a term so derisive that it can scar a little boy for life. A child can lie, steal, cheat and utter the most appalling oaths and no one gets too upset — but let a couple of tears fall and he will be shunned by parent, teacher and friend. And when he grows up he will make absolutely sure that his children are guilty of no such weakness. The prejudice reproduces itself like a reactor.

I cry frequently, and so does my whole family. Not the whole time, but on special occasions, emotional moments, partings, pride at someone else's small triumph, extreme joy, dog dying, Miss Christie getting her man when all had appeared lost, Auld Lang Syne on New Year's Eve.

Apart from this failing (if failing it be) we are a tough, resolute quartet; only at high points and low points is there a risk that the great warm tears may emerge. We are all well aware of the danger, and have been known to catch each others's eyes knowingly and shamefacedly across crowded rooms. I have invented all sorts of techniques for hiding this abnormality — such as quick work with the handkerchief camouflaged by a fit of coughing, or immense stoopings and doing up of shoe-laces, brushing the cheek with the sleeve as it is done.

Crying is infectious, and in moments of stress it spreads like measles. On the night of President Kennedy's death the three of us were sitting at home, too stunned to talk. Our youngest was at the cinema in Wisbech when the black news was flashed on the screen. He left the cinema, bicycled home, threw open the doors, said "Have you heard" and burst into tears. So did we all.

There was an awful moment — not in the same bleak depths — when we were saying goodbye last year to my wife's brother and his family at the station at Sidney, Nebraska. The four of us were at the train window uttering brave last-minute irrelevances, wishing the train would move off and get the thing over, tears dragging down four pairs of cheeks. Suddenly we realised that my four in-laws were in exactly the same state. And as they realised it too, we burst into gales of embarrassed laughter, and that is how we left one another.

Crying is not only infectious — it evidently runs in families. Perhaps my upright, stoic and coldly military father had his soft moments too. If he did, I never knew of them.

An extreme example of the infectiousness of this shortcoming happened to me at a Cup Final, the one in which Manchester United played and lost directly after the Munich air crash. Seated beside me were two delicious Manchester girls, decked all over with red rosettes, tassels and pom-poms. When their heroes came to get their runners-up medals and we were all standing and clapping as though our lives depended on making them hear, I glanced at the two girls. Tears were pouring down each lovely face. I was not sad that Manchester had lost and I had recovered from the shock of the air crash — but the next thing I knew was that I was having to make great play with a

sneezing fit so that there was no danger of the world seeing —
you know what.

It is only at the cinema that the confirmed tear-dropper can
relax. In the comforting darkness as the heartbreak unfolds, it
is possible to sniff away quietly to oneself, disturbing nobody
and free from any danger of being branded a baby. My wife —
an infinitely tougher and more resolute character than myself —
sits beside me, similarly committed, dread secret concealed.
Right at the end of *Breakfast at Tiffany's* (I remember with no
joy) there was an overwhelmingly emotional scene involving a
cat. Suddenly the film was over and there we both were, in the
bright light, exposed to the world, cheeks damp, eyes red.

There is, very likely, a wholesome explanation. Perhaps we
have faulty release mechanisms on our tear ducts. I like to
think that it is because we all feel deeply and have emotions
that are active. If we drop a hammer on our toes or break a leg,
our upper lips are as stiff as anyone could require. We are not
babies in every respect.

I had the enormity of our family failing vividly brought home
to me the other week. My eldest son had gone to America for
eight months. We had not got the courage to go down to the
boat to see him off. We knew too well what would happen to us
all. So we arranged for my mother, who lives near
Southampton, to go to the Ocean Terminus to say goodbye.

She telephoned that evening. "It was nice seeing him and he
has good manners," she said, then added darkly, "I'm afraid I
left him in tears — but probably America will toughen him
up". Little does she know.

Equestrian World

At the risk of creating hitherto undreamed-of demands upon my postwoman, I would like to explain what it is that makes me just the smallest bit touchy about the equestrian world. I confess that I think that the clothes horse-people sometimes wear are odd — more suited to funerals than sport. I confess that some of those girls one sometimes sees, bowlers pressed down over their eyes, hair in buns, curdling the blood of 17-hand horses by the sheer venom of their language, are a little forbidding; but I also know that, separated from their saddles, the same ladies can be seen in the evenings to be deliciously feminine and dulcet-voiced.

Even the ferocious top-hatted men at whom one shudders at meets, cracking whips and glowering down on pedestrians from about 20 feet are, I am assured, quite different at home — devoted to their small pets, dedicated to making neat pieces of pottery while the hi-fi plays Brahms. What really makes me shy just a little at the sound of clip-clop (even after many years as the husband of a riding club chairman) is a sinister little horse person whose ghost still clanks around my hall.

When I was six or so, our family gave shelter to a small, woolly black pony called Joey. Having no bicycle at the time, I was able to perceive an efficient means of transport between our house and a small stream a mile distant, in which I caught roach and very occasionally a paste-eating trout. I was given a couple of lessons in sitting on the animal by a neighbour, a steeplechase jockey called Jack Rennison, and was thenceforth able to make use of my fishing taxi.

It never crossed my mind that riding was an obscure business until one week-end Barber came. He was then a very newly

commissioned officer in one of the cavalry regiments, one of my
mother's baser friends, and clearly completely tuned-in to
horses. I made the fatal mistake of saddling Joey and getting on
him while within sight of his small blackberry eyes; within
seconds I was, apparently, within the jurisdiction of the Army
Acts. Before I knew what had overtaken me I was trotting
round in circles with Barber barking at me from the centre,
adjusting my stirrups, tugging at my reins, pushing me from
side to side and roaring orders and instructions at me as
though I were a squadron of Hussars. I put up with it for 20
minutes or so and then, without permission, dismissed myself,
rode away, turned the pony into the orchard and went into the
house to initiate an urgent Bicycle Fund. It was many years
before I was able to shake off the trauma.

What might be called my second round with Barber took
place much later. It left even deeper scars. A set of
unpredictable military calculations had set me down, dusty and
not at all kempt, in Cairo one Saturday night. This event was
immediately celebrated by the garrison sergeant-major electing
me with unheard-of speed to a church parade the very next
morning. I did my best with the clothing I had. I brushed my
khaki drill, and even washed some of the oilier patches. I
plastered my boots with polish. I had, none the less, to concede
that in terms of immaculacy I fell far short of the other
churchgoers.

Of this fact I became deeply conscious when across the
parade-ground to inspect me stepped the immaculately turned-
out Barber. Though slightly shrunken and wearing now a large,
black moustache, it was, to my horror, unmistakably he,
already one of the Army's most senior captains. In his hand was
a whip, with which he kept smacking his boots — which were a
gleaming mahogany blaze. All his badges sparkled, and he was
very, very clean. I drew him like a magnet. "This thing", he
said pointing at me with his whip and wishing it was a barge

pole, "is filthy. Send it away and put it on a charge."

As this effectively put paid to a number of long-cherished hopes and plans, while I spent my next seven days denied the delights of Cairo, I put him on top of my list of candidates for immediate decapitation when the time came. Curiously enough, though I was never able to carry out my main intention, I had, later, a small moment of triumph. I came upon him in Germany, still shiny, still clean; but by then I was a rank higher than he. "Good morning, Barber" I said with a kindly nod as I passed quickly by — and saw his eyes glitter with perplexity and frustration.

This traces the full circle. It is certainly not horse-people as a whole that make me tremble. Horses themselves, though not in my view as intelligent and reliable as they are good to look at, fill me with no extraordinary foreboding. The simple answer is — and the reason too, why I consistently refuse all offers of mounts — that I know that the moment I am in the saddle, out of the shadows old Barber will emerge, greying moustache twitching, cavalry voice in full spatter, small, sinister, blackberry eyes gleaming with anticipation.

Talking to the Dog

Sometimes I feel a quick pang of shame when I find myself doing it. Once or twice I have realised suddenly, that I am being watched, with apparent resignation, by my whole family, hands on hips, eyebrows lifted, expressions as if to say "What will he be doing next?" I stop and slip back to conventional language, but I know that at any moment I may relapse again.

The truth is that I cannot talk to any dog in a normal voice. Some primeval force inside me makes me slur my vowels and crucify my consonants. What emerges is a cross between baby talk, an American imitating a Cockney accent and an old-time Empire Builder advising his house-boy. It is all very well for them to pretend to look aghast. I know that they do it as well, each in his or her particular and individual way.

The relationship between a dog and its family is a delicate one, based on mutual respect and affection. When we were all away for six weeks, eighteen months ago, it was seeing Bodil that we looked forward to most when we returned. Each dog we have had (with one exception) has bewitched us and insinuated itself, with supreme cunning, into the depths of our hearts. All but one have become an integral part of the family.

The only exception was a miniature dachshund called Briar, a brown lozenge-shaped animal small enough to be slipped into the pocket of my wife's jeep coat. He was our first dog and arrived shortly before our first offspring. He became so resentful of the squawling, smelly brat that later received so much nervous attention, that he developed the habit of slipping silently up to our bedroom two or three times a day and lifting his leg against the bedspread. No sanctions, no amount of scattered pepper, could deter him, and we finally handed him over to a dachshund addict.

Next came Banger. A sitter-in sold her to the boys (who by then had reached an impressionable age, but had no idea of the value of money) for 5s. We returned from our party to find ourselves the owners of a cubic cream-coloured ball of fluff. When in later years we found it necessary to reproach her, we were prone to remind her that we had paid through the nose for her.

She was a charming creature, a distillation of pomeranian and spaniel, yet in a mysterious way she appeared to belong to a proper breed, the sort of dog one might easily see surrounded by ecstatic Dog People at Cruft's. Strangers refused to believe that she did not belong to a classy, if rare, species and we invented one or two — Siberian Elk Hound — North Norfolk Fox Harrier — to satisfy them.

She had long, golden hair and looked as though she had just had an expensive rinse, except during one hot summer when we clipped her, leaving just her mane and a pom-pom on the end of her tail. Then she looked like a cheerful, conceited mutation, out of the lion family. She was immensely intelligent and exploited with ease every human weakness. She had her own way throughout her life and could do anything except go for a walk on her lead. We never succeeded in curing her of walking on her hind legs, holding the lead with her fore-paws. She only did it for a giggle, of course.

She was desperately in love with the postman and her ecstatic screams told us each morning when the post had arrived. We all talked to her in voices from the back of our throats, with exaggerated jaw movement. Some of our friends found this odd but Banger understood perfectly.

In her later years Banger was joined by a whippet whom we called Equil, whose father had the imposing name of Allways Winged-foot Running Fox. He was a small golden athlete of a dog whom we once timed beside the car at 32 m.p.h. He was slightly overshadowed by Banger's dynamism but they made an unusual pair. There was no danger of a somewhat curious family, Banger having had an operation after her fourth litter in 18 months. We used to speak to Equil in squeaky voices, rather mincingly.

They both died within a month, one sad spring. Soon afterwards a friend who lived in a small house with a small garden and a cluster of small children asked us if we would take his Lemon Labrador puppy, who had proved too obstreperous for his particular set-up. Before we knew it, we had inherited, free, Bodil.

It took her a year to become attached to us, a year during which she remained well-mannered but offhand, showing enthusiasm only when she saw her former owner. Since she made up her mind about us she has become slavishly adoring and infinitely anxious to please. Her greatest moment of the day is when she runs to the edge of the estate to greet the postman or the paperman and tears back with a mouthful of letters or newspapers. We are still trying to teach her to bring them to our bedroom and not to leave them in her basket.

Such rounded beauty and talent demands and gets — a special kind of language, a round-mouthed pouting rigmarole full of Bs and Ps, and the frequent use of the word Gorgeous, pronounced Garjus. She takes in every word we utter.

For some reason I have an even stranger way of talking to our horse, but I had better end the confession at this point before damage is done to a reputation for sober reliability.

Paler Than Cream

It is difficult to describe Bodil's beauty. Darker than milk but paler than cream, there can only be a fraction of an inch here, a degree or two there, that distinguish her from all the other dogs of the same breed (but that, of course, is all there is that distinguishes the Grace Kellys and Julie Christies from other members of their sex). Yet of her exceptional grace and charm there can be no doubt. People gasp when they see her. Strangers cannot keep their hands off her. A walk with her produces an entourage of admirers. Once at a point-to-point I had almost to fight my way to the car through a mass of crooning, sighing dog-people.

To begin with, I was not sure that beauty was sufficient. She was charming enough, obliging and well mannered and almost disdainfully obedient. But I had the feeling occasionally of a certain shallowness — the sensation a husband may have when he discovers that deliciousness is his bride's only quality. It was only when her former owner came to see us, as I have said, that she really lit up — the rapturousness of her greeting on those occasions was moving.

After a full year it became clear that we had at last taken his place, and that she had finally decided that we were wonderful too. Now when her former owner comes, he gets no more than courtesy and good manners demand.

Ever since the end of that first year the relationship has thrived. She is the constant companion of the whole family, shooting with one, following another on her horse, fishing with another, holidaying with us all. It was, in fact, on a holiday in Scotland that we realised that she was not quite out of the top drawer. After stumbling upon her first hare, there followed a

frantic three-quarters of a mile chase and the whole valley rang with her high-pitched yips. Our host gravely told us that a correctly bred Labrador would never make noises like that.

Although there are occasions — for example when she is being a little too queenly for her own good — when we have to remind her that in her background there is a touch of the terrier-brush, we have not allowed this revelation to upset our idyll. It may account for and explain the fact that she is the poorest of gun dogs, exasperatingly liable to retrieve a stick instead of a bird. Her fishing is little better, possibly for the same reason. She reacts sharply when one is caught but only gazes longingly at the catch — bearing in mind too obviously the possibility of leftovers for herself. As a housedog she has the most intimidating bark but not the faintest sign of a bite. Her beauty and her overwhelmingly affectionate and generous nature remain her two greatest assets.

Our duty to the community was clear from the start. It was our task to ensure that her unique characteristics were passed on to succeeding generations. After much heart-searching we made plans for her introduction to another Labrador whose pedigree and temperament were beyond reproach.

Bodil, however, had other ideas, and before anything could be done about it she had swiftly selected and become betrothed to a dog who happened to be passing down the lane in pursuit of a tractor. Our information about him is scanty, but the one vital thing was that he appeared to be of the same breed and colour. We put the best possible face on the whole affair and awaited the events that would follow 57 days later.

She started having her puppies at eight o'clock in the evening and by next morning was the proud if somewhat startled mother of a family of nine. Details of this bonanza were leaked to the postman and the paperman and from them the news spread like a thunderstorm. Shortly after breakfast the four children of our neighbours arrived "to see Bo's pups" and from that moment and for the rest of the day, she received with obvious pleasure an unbroken flow of visitors.

By lunch-time thirty-one well-wishers had called to see her and hers. At 1.20 p.m. the Vet (her former owner, incidentally) called to reduce her family to a manageable four, and by three o'clock each of the survivors had been spoken for, reserved and become a postponed-delivery Christmas present. By the same evening there was a pleading, strident waiting-list of seven.

The story of the lady who assaulted a passer-by who had been rash enough to make a disparaging remark about her dog — "fleabag" was the word that was used— should have surprised no one. The love of dog-owners for their dogs often verges on the unbalanced. Parents are frequently quite critical of their children. Even horse-people will occasionally admit to frailties in their loved ones — but the quantities of very goose-like creatures that are regarded ecstatically as swans by dog-lovers are quite beyond counting. It is nice to realise that our own judgment is sober, balanced and confirmed by the general public.

Holiday Camps

The time draws near at last when the nose can be prised from the grindstone, the burdens of life tossed away and the ensuing fortnight can be squandered in joyous irresponsibility.

But before the moment comes when the loaded car heads its way west, many complex preparations must be made. Evidence of the coming holiday will start to be manifested in complex piles all over the house — heralding the coming festivity like holly before Christmas.

Sometimes (as I prowl determinedly about, preparing) I begin to think that I have missed my real calling — a top echelon military administrator, moving the 9th/10th Light Infantry to Singapore and back, without overlooking a single pith helmet, or casually organising a quick invasion. Quarter-Master General Sir David (Bizzy) Barr, a legend in his time . . .

Back to reality, my preparations fall into two main camps. Camp 1 is established in our bedroom, to which on D-Day minus 14, I stagger with a large trunk which is left open on the floor. My wife (who can pack in 15 minutes and never overlook a hair-pin) has given up the struggle to prevent this. Day by day I cast into it (I don't do the folding and fitting) my fortnight's necessities — a couple of shirts one morning, socks and handkerchiefs the next, two old pairs of trousers the next. It might appear haphazard but the object is achieved with computer-like accuracy. Over the weeks the holidaymaker's complete wardrobe is built up — clothes for getting wet in, clothes for drying out in, clothes for keeping the cold out, bright sparkling combinations for talks with the girls at the reception desk, summer stuff in case the sun shines. If we took

a wrong turning and ended in Antarctica I would be equipped to survive interminably.

Camp 2 is the really important pile, though — the fun pile I build in the corner of the dining room, traditionally in the same corner, under the cupboard by the window — a spreading extending pile that must considerably cut down the task of keeping the floor clean.

Into the fun pile goes at once the fishing tackle. The very sight of it, waiting there expectantly, brightens my breakfasts. It always starts, sensibly, with just one rod and all that goes with it. It ends (as my mind grows more expansive and I allow for all the weather possibilities) with at least three, with all vital accoutrements.

This particular group can become endless; it takes all the General's calm foresight to make sure that nothing is forgotten — yet that nothing unnecessary is taken. I will never forget the moment when I stood beside the swirling waters of a pool full of leaping salmon and found that I had everything with me but the rod's top joint — which was still snug in a shop at home 500 miles away, awaiting collection.

Fishing tackle may make up the flesh of the dining room pile, but there are plenty of bones as well. Books to read, the hotel's letter confirming the booking, green insurance card, dog lead and dog food, tin- and bottle-openers, address book, collection of post cards from other holidays (contrary, we send Hay-on-Wye cards from Kerry, Views of the Post Office, Elm from Scotland) golf clubs, binoculars, road maps, chess set (for days when more than an inch of rain falls) — a welter of holiday necessities that can be calmly assembled in two weeks but which would cause even the sharpest administrator to furrow his brow if attempted on the eve of D-Day.

While building Camps 1 and 2 the energies must also be diverted (however taxing it may be) to the other necessities sudden absence involves. P.C. Upjohn must be secretly informed of the empty house. The milk must be stopped. Wally Berry must be persuaded to cease delivering his early morning piles of newsprint. Someone must be found who, in return for three eggs a day, will give the chickens their morning wheat and their lunchtime mash. Two weeks' supply of both must be laid in. Willing girls must be bribed to water the pampered horses, even in the knowledge that the saddles and bridles will be locked away. House keys must be distributed so that emergency access can be gained — and so that the craftsman who is coming to paper the walls of the downstairs lavatory can get in and out.

And of course the spending money must be drawn and gathered together — which includes the task of taking my pint mug containing all spare 1, 2 and 5p pieces since Christmas to the bank, under armed escort if necessary — and turning the contents into — I hope and trust — at least eleven crisp pound notes.

By the last night, when the gardening tools scattered during the summer throughout the length and breadth of the garden have been gathered and locked away, I begin to know what Sir Douglas Haig meant when he entered a note in his diary about one of his corps commanders who had lost 70,000 of his men in quick time and without gain. "He looked tired" wrote the Field Marshal, "and had evidently passed through an anxious time."

Still, if I can fit the contents of all the Camps in the car, leave nothing behind and still leave room for the dog, I am sure it will prove to have been worth while.

Fishing Mania

In my younger and more foolish days I used to dream of having a Fishing Wife all of my own. I conjured up all kinds of visions of the delicious creature who would accompany me, hand in hand, from river to river, pool to pool. Wherever I would go the little pal would come too. We would land each other's fish, solve each other's problems, rejoice in each other's triumphs. It did not fortunately work out that way.

There is of course something a little forbidding about the uniform of fishing. It is hard for the most adorable girl to look too enticing in a pair of waders. There is little that is attractive about an anorak or fishing coat. Even the act of casting is not something that many women find easy to perform with grace. They are built for all sorts of other sports but not, except in rare cases, for fishing.

I was never, in fact, in any real danger of losing my heart to a fishing girl because I never met an attractive one — though I am sure there must have been some glorious ones about. Those whom I met were, in the main, rugged kilted creatures, grandmothers for the most part with deep voices and humiliating copious funds of knowledge. The younger ones, I suspect, knew of all sorts of occupations in which they would show to better advantage.

The woman in a fisherman's life is so vital that not only the choosing but also, subsequently, the manner of playing her deserves the most careful thought and attention. The great, long contest between dedication to fishing and family if badly fought can end in disaster. Few women marrying fishermen have any clear idea of the obligations that they are taking on. Many, I suspect, beam benevolently upon their angling fiancé, firmly believing that a year or two as a family man will cure him of THAT. From such thinking springs the seeds of broken marriages, abandoned children and called-in mortgages. It is really essential for the girl marrying the real genuine dyed-in-the-wool obsessive fisherman to come to terms with the problem and to do so quickly.

My wife, as you know, comes from the U.S.A. and Americans, as we all know, have the strangest ideas about fishing. They use Poles. The whole family takes the car to a pond and sits beside it pulling out catfish. Afterwards they have a barbecue. The kind of madness which strikes me and my fellow sufferers, which draws us to water ten hours a day, day after holiday day, and which leaves us in the end totally unsatisfied, is unknown in her native land.

It must, alas, have come as something of a shock on our Scottish honeymoon when the fishing did not end. Madly in love as I was, I was suffering for the first time from the awful malaise that is caused by the desire to be in two places at once. One of them was beside a river, burn or loch.

We had had in fact an unsatisfactory day, fishing — in the loch opposite the hotel, up the burn that fed it and finally from a boat on Loch Catrine (the Sir Walter Scott towed us out, she rowed us back). At that moment (it had rained åll day) I realised that the river at Callander should have a little colour in it. There could clearly be the chance of a sea-trout or even a salmon. We had no car but I managed to make an arrangement with the head waiter for the hire of two bicycles. Callander was little more than 5 miles away — and a lot of the road was downhill. "Let's get moving, darling," I said, my voice loaded with the affection I felt for the tall and beloved creature who had resigned herself to me.

There was a long, silent pause — one of the few pauses that have ever come between us. "Take your bicycle," she said (and in American it sounds like a machine made in one of the

remote planets). "Bicycle yourself off to wherever you want —
but I've had all the water today that I can take." At that
moment I heard distinctly the sound of clinking chains, the
noise of doors slamming. I realised — for the very first time,
perhaps — that I was married and under the clearest obligation
to compromise with my mania. That night we stayed, no sulks,
no grievances, contentedly in the hotel.

The spirit of compromise, as my wife would be the first to
admit, can be overdone. A year or two later we went on holiday
to a place that was miles from any conceivable type of fishing.
We sat at bars and drank; we wandered through woods, we
looked at endless statues. We even photographed the scenery.
We both vowed that we would never do it again. I was neither
mean nor detestable — but I was certainly frustrated, and the
spirit of frustration spreads like a weed.

We have never again gone on a non-fishing holiday. We have
learnt that there are many little heavens that can still be found,
superb unpublicised places to stay at where the food is good,
the young are welcome, where wives can find real enjoyment —
and where good rivers wind near by, in which the husband can
sublimate himself in search of salmon, sea-trout or trout.

Achilles' Heel

My wife, accomplished, talented and habitually able to achieve any peak she decides to climb, is certainly one of the bottom ten Lady Golfers in the United Kingdom. She plays regularly — at least four times a year without fail — yet despite this her game shows little detectable improvement — or even promise. I find it comforting that she has this Achilles' heel, but there are a number of explanations.

She has not got much in the way of equipment of course — but this is appropriate. It would be wholly unsuitable for a golfer of her calibre to have a real bag and perhaps a dozen clubs and knitted numbered headcovers (or whatever they are called) or even a coloured umbrella. She carries her three clubs with a certain élan, dropping her unwanted ones while the other is in use.

She has a wooden shafted driver (dug out of a friend's attic and rescued from a bonfire). The shaft curves delicately and there is a bird's nest of loose string above the head. Next, there is Judy Hodgson, a very expensive No. 3 Iron given to her by a cured patient of that name. Finally a No. 8 which she bought herself, her sole golfing capital expenditure. On the odd occasion when she reaches a green she borrows a putter.

It is her technique that is her undoing. Her eyesight is good. She's a tall, athletic girl, strong enough if need be to fell me effortlessly with a left or right hook. Her handicap is her insistent application of a method uniquely her own — and nothing can change her.

She stands poised by the ball, lifts the club slowly upwards till it points to the sky, then suddenly (as though carrying out a swift assassination) strikes the ball a furious downward crack.

Usually this drives it deep into the turf but every now and then (especially when it is wet) the ball shoots forward as though pressed between a giant finger and thumb.

For her a fifty yard carry is a moment of glory, even a twenty yarder is by no means unsatisfactory to her. She enjoys her golf immensely, counting her shots by the half dozen. "I went round in fifty", she will say with pride at the ninth hole. Only a select few recognise this as a score of 300. Playing in her company is thoroughly enjoyable. She never gets angry or ruffled — in fact, there is a serenity about her game that would surprise an onlooker unlucky enough not to know her.

Moreover, my own 45 degree slices and pulls that nevertheless travel a hundred yards or so are by comparison Gary Player-type shots, drawing from her gasps of admiration. It is all very good for the morale.

From all this there is a lesson to be learned. Until I, too, became a regular golfer I was under the banal and commonplace impression that Lady Golfers were immensely efficient — and immensely ugly — thick women of great power. Now that I share golf courses with them more frequently I realise that they are, one and all, gleamingly attractive but savagely incompetent. Though there is clear evidence that one or two are good at the game, such tyros are rare as forty pound salmon or Black Admirals or Snow Buntings. The remainder are decorative but beyond hope and, sad to say, it would appear that this matters. Snowed under by equipment, lovely brows wrinkled by the effort of remembering the eighty-one things the professionals have been dinning into their innocent heads, they become gloomily frustrated and soured. If only they would realise that a golf swing is a ridiculous thing, contrary to nature and contravening every law of impulse and impact, they might become more philosophic. A woman is just not built for swing-ing. The very convexes and concaves that are her triumphant charm make the exercise grotesque, if not impossible.

So my message to all golfing sweethearts is to give up the unequal struggle to break a hundred. Even if every lady's tee was shifted forward another fifty yards the task would for the majority be hopeless. Let one and all adopt, instead, the gay and carefree attitude of my wife. Once all are resigned contentedly to count in sixes, the joy of playing will speedily return — and those beloved brows will at last become smooth and serene again.

Bronzed and Fit

Back from late holidays, bronzed and muscular. Carrying not an ounce of surplus flesh, despite the succulences of Ernie Evans's cooking in County Kerry. Rejuvenated by the active life in the sun and wind, complexion firm, step jaunty and vibrant, mind blown clear of the worries of the year, a man resiliently ready for everything the next 49 weeks may have in store, ten years ageing effortlessly cast away.

New Year's Eve is an absurd time to take stock and make resolutions. Body and mind will already have had eight weeks of dark nights, cold, wet and fog — to say nothing of the excesses of Christmas. Morale will be low enough to affect judgment and outlook. No, the time for the new plan, the sharp, discerning look at the shape of things to come, is when one is at one's peak, fit and hard and relaxed after a holiday.

Three items on the debit side can be coolly faced. First, the deteriorating eyesight. Now, holiday or no holiday, two pairs of glasses need to be carried about in the coat pocket, mixing aggravatingly with diary, money, cigarettes, matches and unanswered letters. One pair is needed to decipher any small print — and even to dial a telephone number with certainty. The other becomes necessary when driving in bad light to enable clear identification to be made of oncoming traffic at more than 80 yards range.

Next, there is the creaking knee-cap that has started to splutter and groan each time I bend it. Finally, there is the wobbly tooth — a new burden — which creates problems each time I bite an apple. No good going to the dentist for respite. He has already spoken words of doom about the future of my teeth. All in all, though, things could be very much worse and I am duly thankful.

Comparatively fit, then, I face the coming months with quiet confidence. The clear brain will cope sharply and efficiently with every problem, dipping lavishly into the capital of experience. At four o'clock each evening (a time at which, three weeks ago, I was failing to conquer the temptation to drop off to sleep) I will be initiating new and exciting ventures. At 6 I will be thinking springily of the evening's activities — devoted, I vow, to good works, to aiding the community, as well as to modest pleasure.

The drive, the decisiveness, the careful, highly organised mode of living, will also have a speedy effect on the family's finances, shattered as they at present are by a pile-up of hotel bills, travelling expenses and large genial rounds of drinks. There must be time too for activities of a wife-preserving nature, for painting the spare bedroom, for preparing the garden for its winter sleep, for putting away, properly greased and cleaned, all the tools and machines. Improving books will be read, smoking will be diminished, rich food and alcohol eliminated, stimulating lectures attended.

On top of all this (and time can always be found with care and foresight) fitness must be maintained — there must be long walks, jogs before breakfast, breathing exercises, bending and stretching (with permission from my knee) perhaps even cold baths. Looked at from my present crystal-clear peak, it is going to be absurdly simple to avoid this year becoming as much of a mess as last. By next September, I will start my well-earned vacation looking tanned and feeling resilient and youthful.

I have this minute completed a conversation with a friend who shared the last days of my holiday with me. "Was it you," he asked, "who was fishing the roadside pool by the sawmill on Saturday morning?" Remembering the skill with which I had performed, the long, graceful, effortless casting, I agreed that it was. The admiration of a knowledgeable passer-by might easily have been excited.

"I thought it might have been," replied my friend, looking happy. "I spoke to someone who told me that an elderly balding man had been flogging the pool and I wondered if it could have been you."

It's a very good thing that I am feeling resilient.

Twentieth Anniversary

One of our favourite family occupations is the celebration of anniversaries. Annual ones rate somewhere between a birthday and Christmas. Five, ten, twelve and a half and fifteen year anniversaries have been excuses for celebrations that bordered on the spectacular. When we were first married we even had small monthly token acknowledgments of the importance of the day, but the years have taken their toll of these, though we usually manage to remember to say "Happy Anniversary" on the tenth of each month.

Of all the past festivities those that we held at the end of twelve and a half years were the most outstanding. The evening started quietly, but after a particularly good dinner we decided to visit a mature but eligible bachelor friend. So pleased was he at the thought of anyone wanting to celebrate an eighth of a century that he pulled out of his air-raid shelter a bottle of 1896 brandy that his grandfather had given him. It was four o'clock on the first morning of the second eighth of our century before we returned home. Now we have moved gently up to the eve of our twentieth year.

A twentieth wedding anniversary gets no particular status. It is not silver, diamond or gold, and certainly not copper. Paper, probably, or cardboard, but to us it seems crucial. Given normal production times, by the end of twenty years one's family is already grown up, looking energetically at careers, thinking thoughts of independence, gazing at roads along which they can race without parents at their elbows.

We are close to the time when the house will become silent — a lull before the storm of grandchildren. It is a dike that all parents must cross, but it is not one that fills me with any pleasant anticipation. The prospect of small, helpless and possibly smelly grandchildren is one that I find unexciting. I shall be a very irritable grandparent indeed.

A strange, ineradicable and highly commercialised part of courtship and marriage is the repeated emphasis on the good looks and vital statistics of those involved. No song is ever written about an ugly girl (though the novel writers occasionally allow their men to be "craggy" or "ugly in a handsome way" or "rugged"). The heroines of the stage and the films are never fat. Physical charm and true romance appear to go hand in hand.

Looking at all this from the peaks of twenty great years, it seems totally illogical that couples should continually be staking their future upon attributes that have nothing to do with character, endurance, stability, energy or honesty. I have already described how I first saw my wife in a crowded Services club in Germany, and before I had spoken to her had made up my mind to marry her. Could any judgment based on this sort of chemistry have been more hazardous and less likely to be followed by so many happy years?

We had only known each other for four weeks when we were married. We were terribly sure, completely mature and infinitely wise. We looked sorrowfully on those of our friends who suggested that we were rushing it. Had we waited another three months — or nine — we would, we now realise, have been no wiser. It is only after the novelties of the first part of marriage and the onset of the routine and the humdrum and the day-to-day pressures that the deep personal discoveries are made.

We each realised by that time that the person we had married was not at all the same person that we thought we had married. It was only by an explosion of peerless good fortune that we felt the same affection for the reality that we had felt for the myth. The gamble of marriage can only be made acceptable by the fact that people are basically unselfish, kind and good — proof indeed of a theory that the only people we thoroughly dislike are those whom we do not know. We would surely even warm to some of the politicians if we were better acquainted with them.

This coming milestone must, between parties, be a moment of stocktaking. Already the days seem a little longer than they did; the garden bigger; the traffic wardens more boyish; the tempo quicker. People whom we like to regard as nearly contemporary are beginning to tell us how young we look, kindly if with a touch of condescension. Some of the burnish has undoubtedly vanished from the brass.

But speaking personally — if my poor wife has been able to tolerate for all this time my untidiness, my occasional bad humour, my various unjustified enthusiasms, my laziness about washing up and my insistence on holidays spent in the middle of salmon rivers, then our lives need not deteriorate during the next two decades, and we might be able to edge into old age with the same busy and delicious surge that has made the first twenty years pass so much too quickly.

The Birds Have Flown

So the Kiddiewinks have gone. The feathers have been grown and the nest is empty. There had been a period before, when they were both away, when (after our hand had been forced) the family was enmeshed in a short stretch of boarding school education. That soon ended, thanks to fortuitous eleven-plusses, and it was not long before we were all sleeping under the same roof again. Now they have both scattered to their respective seats of learning and we, the parents, face with no great relish the silence — the comparative silence — of a house abandoned by half its occupants.

This time, of course, it is final. There will be periods — week-ends and Christmas holidays — when they are back, but the continuity is gone forever and the inevitable pattern is set. We would not have it otherwise.

The differences are curious. Our highly prized radiogram, accustomed to hard work, thumping out B.B.C. or hillocks of a dozen L.P.s, looks at us in silent reproach. We do not seem to have the inclination to set up yet the old rich mixtures of Alpert, Beatles, Conniff and Piaf — interspersed with unlikely blends of Mozart, Wagner and Dvořák. The washing machine which had till now poured forth tubful after tubful of clean, dry clothing suffers only occasional interruptions in its holidays. The refrigerator, loaded normally with handy snacks and raided from dawn to dusk, sits in dignity, its diminished contents static. The rooms upstairs, so recently a bedlam of clothes-changing and bath-taking and in-and-outing, remain depressingly quiet. Drawers all over the house that had spent their time half open are now neatly closed. Our cars, which once neither of us seemed to have much prospect of using, remain outside, looking almost stately in their inactivity. Only Dark Red, their £52 10s. 1951 Riley, still unsold, remains as a stark reminder of the energy that went into its joint purchase. It is as though a giant spring has unwound.

It is not, to be sure, the end of the world. In the winter that is coming — and to be perfectly candid, all subsequent winters — there are going to be ample opportunities for doing many of the things there did not seem to be time for before. We shall be able to organise our lives efficiently and progressively. We shall start playing bridge again, racy, brilliant bridge comfortably interspersed with a flood of conversation. We will read the books we should have read before and catch the new ones from the reviews. We will take improving courses at night school and learn all about concrete mixing and metallurgy and the Common Market — sharpening our brains to razor keenness. We will read "Radio Times" in detail, marking down the stimulating and informative programmes that somehow in the past we have always missed.

We will invite to supper not only our friends but also all those we had so many good reasons for not inviting in the past. We shall polish floors and paint the bathroom and tidy the garden shed and grease the motor-mower. Shorn of the galloping consumption of food, the countless telephone calls to scattered girl-friends, the lights left gaily on so that the house looked like an ocean liner at night, we will make the housekeeping (scale reduced, of course) last the full seven days. We may even find ourselves able, eventually, to purchase some of those stocks or shares the activities of which lighten the lives of so many. Having been able to cancel "The Racing Specialist" and "The Weekly Tipster", we may find ourselves needing the "Financial Times". We shall become calm and gracious — but interesting and sought after, too, as our minds expand from the books and the night classes.

Those who visit us will carefully wipe their shoes before

coming through the front door and will warmly admire the tidy rooms, the immaculate carpets and the plump, unruffled cushions . . .

The only thing is that it is not working out that way at all. In the first three weeks we have only been at home on four evenings. On those evenings scores of people emerged from the darkness, complaining that we were never in, and turning each one of them into a night of minor revelry. The books are still unopened. The garden shed is chaotic. We have failed to attend a single lecture.

Even so, we thrive on the certainty that Christmas is not, after all, very far away.

Enjoying Winter

It is in November, every year, when I start to think dolefully of the months to come — of the fogs, the cold, the damp, the leafless trees, the brown instead of the green, the ice, the dark mornings, the long evenings. More than a quarter of a year lies between me and the first unarguable whiffs of spring that fly flags for the end of winter. The brightness of October is always a snare and a delusion — nature's last hand with a brilliant house of cards that collapses with the first sharp frost. After that, the blackout.

This, at any rate, is how I have been dealing with winter in the past. A series of hurdles to be scrambled over — shortest day, 21 December, and out with the new diary to trace the slowly increasing light. Interlude in the bleakness for Christmas, at once a buffer against the new year's bills and the originator of many of them. Kindly gestures in January and February as the aconites and then the snowdrops and crocuses emerge. A stolen Saturday or two, if one is lucky, at the early point-to-points and then March, unarguably only 31 days (including a birthday) before the illness is over.

I have recently come to realise that such an attitude is crazy. No one has yet confided in me for how many days and weeks and winters I am, as the saying is, going to be spared. In this particular game, however, even if the numbers are not revealed, the players should all be aware that the rules lay down a strict limit. To write off, each year, a third of the residue is even by my own dim standards unbelievably short-sighted.

My stupidity goes even further. I spend my time in a state of suspended anticipation. Only three more days (or ten, or a month) before the next beacon — the week-end or the answer to a letter or the golf appointment or the fishing season or the cup tie (sadly my own team normally loses interest in cup ties before the summer is finished). When I returned to the Ancient Borough this September after an immensely happy holiday in Ireland I even said, "Only 48 weeks before we are back there." What a confession to have to make. What short-sighted profligacy with a dwindling bank account.

At the risk of making noises like a homespun philosopher, I must shamefacedly admit that only comparatively recently has it sunk into my mind that happiness, unlike less desirable states such as misery or pain, is hard to measure and often even to recognise. I have found it easier to spot as I have grown older, and as I discarded slowly the attitude that it was necessary to be doing something to catch it, that supreme happiness can only be attained by achieving miraculous peaks like opening the batting for England or winning a Nobel Prize. It has been a fortunate adjustment that has coincided with the realisation that no such honours will ever come my way.

Happiness must be especially difficult for the young to discern, when the blisses referred to in every pop song are wearing thin, when the babies are crying and the day is too long and the only hope of relieving the pressure seems to lie in the successful prediction of eight draws. Yet this is what living is about, and from these pressures the seeds of present contentment must be found without keeping the eyes on future oases — like the next holiday, the club dance, the night out with the boys. For all of us, too many good moments slip by unnoticed. We only miss them when they do not return.

There would be splendid rewards for someone who invented a Happiness Indicator, or some small machine which flashed red at moments of contentment — or a golden light that vanished during quarrels or anger or boredom. I believe we would all be surprised how often it flashed red or stayed on. With or without such a machine, a big change is going to take place in my attitude towards this winter. No more anticipation, no more looking forward and ignoring the valuable gaps in between.

I am going to spend a lot of time from now on looking appreciatively at the desolate scenes outside, breathing in great gulps of the delicious dank cold air, revelling in the black mornings — and determinedly avoiding giving a passing thought to next Thursday's party, the dinner in three weeks' time or the four days away from work at Christmas.

Venetian Gates

We have a beautiful pair of Venetian wrought-iron gates that open into the orchard — a tapestry of living, writhing steel, through which I have been passing since I was a clear-eyed, cold-bathing boy. My mother moved them from house to house, and then, when we went to live at Elm (she had bought a house which already had a gate) gave them to us, labelling them and sending them to us by British Road Services.

At first they were hung on two fine oak posts, with a wire fence stretching to the dike on either side, looking as pretentious as a mink coat in a cattle-market. Now that the beech hedge has grown up thick, high and sturdy to span the gaps, they look more fitting. Even so, it would be more appropriate to peer through them at sunken lawns, ornate pools, peacocks, and topiary — rather than a hundred yards of muddy grass and lines of grizzled plum trees leading to a grey and endless Fenland skyline.

My own eye is sleepy when it comes to noticing defects. I can live for ever in a shabby room and never remark the faded paint. A carpet's holes must trip me up before I regard it as less than brand new. Fortunately for us, my wife detects a need for renewal or repair the moment it appears — someone has to maintain standards. Yet it was I, strangely enough, who decided that the rusting gates must have attention. I nominated this as my project for the winter.

One at a time was the plan, as we lifted the left-hand one off its post and staggered with it into the conservatory, propping it up carefully so that it was not likely to fall on any passing child or dog. Then we set about it, a section at a time, two or three evenings a week, with rust remover, sandpaper, files and wire

brushes. To get every grain of rust from a hundred tiny quadrilaterals, steel roses and curlicues would have been a life's work. Though seeing myself already as a craftsman, strong-armed and steady-handed, I was quickly ready to compromise, pragmatic as any politician. We scraped away the peeling paint and the very worst of the rust, The remainder would have to fight its way through undercoat and top-coat, ready to be attacked again in ten years' time.

The old-fashioned craftsmen (they don't come like that, these days) would, of course, have tolerated no such compromise. The 20-century European craftsman, like me, is ready not only to compromise, but to take into use all modern aids — like Aerosol undercoat sprayed from a tin.

The Aerosol was not a success; instead of the paint nestling thickly on every unreachable cranny, the bulk of the tin ended up on the walls, in my lungs, and over my clothes. It hardly stained the gate. So it was back to the old tin and the paint-brushes, and eventually a nice grey gate was lifted back into position, ready for the final dose.

I would finish the job at Christmas, I decided determinedly — a fine, constructive way of spending the holiday. Moreover, on this last lap, not one single part of the pattern, not the shields, nor the roses, nor the tiny combinations of squares would be missed. I started at the top on the Saturday before Christmas, and methodically worked my way downwards, in half-hour spells at the end of most of which my teeth were chattering. By Christmas morning I had completed more than half of one side, and rather less of the other.

All through Boxing Day and the day after I sat there on a three-legged stool, listening to the busy life of the chickens, stared at malevolently by the cockerel (who hates me because I chase him once a fortnight to keep him in his place), brushes busy as knitting-needles, admired by passing members of the family, none of whom, strangely, volunteered to help preserve the heirloom. Only a man who has painted a wrought-iron gate from grey to black can realise how many dimensions it has, how the job from one angle looks perfect, but from another is revealed in endless inches of untouched undercoat.

By the time it was done and I was able to survey with overflowing pride the finished article, my eyes were strained, my back was stiff, my hands were sore, and my skin was covered with black paint ("diamond hard on any steel within ten minutes"), which the heaviest applications of turpentine showed no sign of removing.

And I was only half-way through a deep sigh of relief when I realised that we had not even touched the other gate, hanging there brown and shabby, shown up and humiliated by its shining sister.

It rather looks as if next Christmas may be busy too.

Flights of Fancy

"The B.B.C. on the 'phone," my wife said.

It was one of their Television producers, hoping to brighten his Christmas programme. "Would you be able to give us five minutes", he pleaded. "Just a chat and a few Yuletide wishes. We'll have one of our outside units come along to your place — and you can pop out, do your stuff and then return to your celebrations." Reluctantly I agreed, the call of my public stronger than my infinite weariness. A hundred guineas was neither here nor there — but one's duty was clear . . .

At that moment the pips went for the seven o'clock news and I came back from my other world, a Walter Mitty of the 1970s, with reality thumping at me as the news reader told of thousands being laid off at Dagenham, expressions of optimism from Vietnam, an air disaster and a football match in which all but ten players were ordered off.

So intricate has life become that the only time I can find for my interesting (and, to a psychiatrist, revealing) flights of fancy is from twenty to seven in the morning, lying in bed with the radio turned low, voyaging from the sad little farming programme through to the moment when London takes over, just after the Norwich and Lowestoft Jottings. From that moment the day is on, full strength, tea brewing, post arriving, bath-water flowing.

The topics of course vary, but I frequently wander into situations that involve a close and respectful relationship with the Royal Family. I find myself (for example) at one of the Palace Luncheons. Perfectly dressed (yet relaxed and sufficiently casual to put everyone at their ease) I can be heard answering a spate of questions, explaining this, theorising lightly on that — a great lovable, infectious grin illuminating the slices of wit that tumble from my mouth.

Sometimes it goes a little further — a week-end at Balmoral. Over the port I can see Harold on my right, nodding wisely and wondering if all his pet theories may not after all be ill founded. The Duke has already found a man after his own heart. Later, when we play golf, my screaming drives gain the widest admiration. And as I cast my salmon fly gracefully (and unprecedentedly) to the far bank of the Dee and hear astonished gasps, I turn with the same broad, friendly grin and say in a low, gentle voice, "When you've been doing it all your life, there's really nothing to it . . .".

I do not always wander in such high places. My television experiences I have already touched upon. Sometimes they are more exciting, little extravaganzas with Twiggy on one side and Antonia Fraser on the other, questions asked and brilliantly answered, the studio audience roaring its approval — with a noticeable extra enthusiasm for the man in the middle, the one whose wide, infectious grin seems to outshine the brilliance of his co-stars.

Sometimes I find myself to be the dynamic chairman of one of the Regional Development Councils, coldly tearing to pieces the mediocre and unimaginative contributions of the paid officials, and then with a wide, disarming grin showing how the region should be run. Or the maiden speech at Westminster, with a hostile House and a topic so full of political dynamite that no one else dares mention it. The Speaker calls the House to order and nods to the new Member for the Isle of Ely. Ten minutes later a gale of applause from both sides of the House witnesses that a breakthrough has been made. Ancient Statesmen surreptitiously wipe their eyes as they glimpse a modest but infectious grin when the new Member sits down . . .

As I have already indicated, this peep into a dreamy mind should be easy stuff for the psychiatrists. All sorts of frustrations and repressions would be unerringly pin-pointed by them — but they would be wrong. The explanation is far more trivial and simple — and dates back a few years to the moments after a football match, Reading v Wisbech Town, F.A. Cup, Round 2.

After the game I was having a beer in the Reading Board Room (which in itself is not a bad throwaway line) when a reporter started asking me questions. Another man (a cartoonist, I later discovered) began to draw on a thick pad. Slowly a group of people gathered round us, smiling, friendly and pleasant. Each of my replies produced a round of appreciative chuckles. Was I enjoying my football? "Certainly," I said, "while we keep winning" (laughter). What did I think of today's game? "Neither side should have lost" (murmurs of appreciation).

Later, interview over and countless drinks refused, I began to make my way from the room when I heard the truth. "Whoever was he?" Someone whispered: "Oh, he's Jesse Pye, the Wolves and England centre-forward, who's playing for them now."

That wiped the great wide, lovable, infectious grin off my face . . .

Christmas Cards

Each Christmas our house becomes festooned with Christmas cards. There is never any need for any other decoration. There are cards on the shelves, cards stuck into picture-frames, cards balanced in rows on the tallboy, clusters of cards on the imitation pine pelmets, cards hanging from strings that have been skilfully fixed to the ceiling. In the end we give up trying to find homes for them all and lay them face upwards in a tray like playing-cards before a game of Pelmanism.

They arrive in such quantities during the final days before what the Americans call The Holiday that it is difficult to absorb or appreciate them. "Another U.N. Card", we say as we rip them open, or "The usual lighted candles from the Carrotberries", or "That's the third Three Wise Men on the trot." We are overwhelmed by sheer numbers — due not to an excess of popularity but to a circle that has come close to being mildly vicious.

The only selectivity we apply in dealing with this mass is in the playing of The Front Mantelpiece Game, a little pastime for which I am entirely responsible and which culminates after a series of promotions and demotions in the choice of the best dozen or so for the place of honour on the shelf above the sitting room fire. Subversive elements in the family spend their waking hours removing the apples of my eye and putting in their place a series of robins and sparkling snow scenes and comic Father Christmases, smoking cigars. After a day or two of this, the atmosphere is apt to become tense.

Apart from colour or design or originality, there is also a temptation to grade cards (a) for effort, (b) for none. There is a world of difference between the carefully chosen card, actually signed by the sender, at one end of the scale and the entirely printed one at the other end, a mere circular with the envelope typed by a not-too-busy secretary and the whole bundle whisked through the firm's franking machine. Nevertheless, the harvest of cards has always been one of Christmas's great pleasures — a harvest the gathering of which has involved not only the sender but also ourselves in effort and expense.

Our own cards, until this year, have had one merit. They have been original. For twenty years we have, without artistic talent or creative ability, doggedly designed our own. Looked at as a whole they were mostly corny, seldom clever, rarely attractive. Not one of them ever achieved even the most roomy front mantelpiece. Nevertheless they reflected, in a disturbed and vulgar way, the family's story over the whole two decades.

On Twelfth Night (or as long after 25 December as we can possibly stretch it) we sadly unhitch all the cards and solemnly list every one of them, setting aside as we do so the dozen or so that for one reason or another demand the answer that they will probably not receive before midsummer. It is this list that is the cause of our enormous flood. We keep it in a large stiff-covered book, and by the very nature of the system (with new names added each year) it grows longer and longer. If people go away their names are naturally retained, and only the names of the few who actually grow to detest us are ever removed. Carried on indefinitely, there need have been no limit to the numbers involved.

At some history-making moment one December, we strolled up the lane to deliver our cards to our near neighbours. At the moment they decided to do the same thing and we met half-way, under the lamp-post. There suddenly dawned in the minds of the four of us a realisation of the extreme stupidity of the whole exercise as we sheepishly exchanged envelopes. We resolved there and then that this year we would only send cards to the people who live a long way off and whom we see too infrequently.

What happens next is going to be interesting. Either we will receive the full flood and guiltily decorate the house in this manner for the final time — or we shall receive only a handful. It will then become crystal clear that for years people have only been sending us cards out of a sense of irritated obligation — after receiving ours. But my real worry is whether I shall remain sufficiently strong minded. Faced by the usual delicious onslaught, I can see myself rushing madly to the printers and spending Christmas Eve poring over the stiff-covered book and feverishly addressing envelopes. Besides, I happen to have had a brilliant idea for this year's card.

Days of Reckoning

Looking back with clear January eyes, I realise that we must have been mad, raving mad. It was as though, almost a whole month before the day, we had been seized with a frenzy. We made lists; we made frantic telephone calls; we had haggard family conferences. "What should we give Bill? . . . Whatever can we find for Eric? . . . We dare not forget Dick . . . and what if Lindy weighs in with her bottle of Attleborough sherry and has had nothing from us?" The pressures were overwhelming.

And for the two of us, no better. "But what do you want? Surely there's something you're longing to have?" (Yet all the time we don't really want to know or tell. Opening the totally unexpected Christmas present, the one which we realise with surprise is exactly what we had been hoping for, that is the true success.)

All the other duties mounted as the days swept by — the cards to the people who would be offended if they were not sent them, as well as to those with whom it is a yearly pleasure to exchange greetings — the food, the booze, the decorations, all the extras needed to fill and keep filled the stomachs of the houseful, as well as of the people who were sure to drop in — to say nothing of the people whom I had asked (in the euphoria of a Sunday party) and forgotten about.

We shudder in retrospect at the sheer magnitude of the operation, while saluting sadly the efficiency and organisation needed to bring it off. The streets and market places during the final run-in, that last savage lap, teemed with people infected in the same way, parcels clutched and slung and wheeled and embraced, expressions of undiluted good will by no means universal. Every journey home for both of us became cluttered with the wrapped impedimenta of Christmas-tide and much unwrappable impedimenta (like turkey and holly and brussels sprouts) as well. In the very last hours the fever had a final upward surge, resulting in unimaginable insanity — more of this (in case we ran out) and even more of that (in case we found ourselves with nothing in reserve). All economic sense vanished — smashing eleven careful months' household budgeting in a shower of tinsel and artificial snow. A 200-day siege would have been simpler to provide for.

When at last the holly wreath was in place, the cards displayed brightly, the coloured lights hoisted into the fir tree, the Christmas tree decorated, the piles of parcels neatly heaped, the food stacked where it was most likely to remain fresh until needed, the bottles arranged at the ready ("I've just remembered we haven't got anything for the dog, so I'll dash up to town for a plastic crackling meat flavoured bone") — when all was finally prepared — we sat with exhausted stares waiting for the guests, for the postman ("hadn't we better get to the Bank before it closes for his Christmas Box and the dustman's and the milkman's and all the others?"), for the people we think may drop in, for the moment when, as if at the blast of a whistle, it all began. The week's housekeeping had already been drawn three times — but indiscretion had gone far beyond this. At the bookshop, the clothing shop, the drink store, the stationer's and the grocer's, there were some very, very nasty last-minute ledger-entries which would make the postman's future visits matters of regret rather than of happy expectation.

The evening of sober reckoning arrived soon after New Year's Eve. On the once-loaded sideboard, there are two half bottles of deteriorating red plonk, an inch and a half of port, a miniature of Cointreau and a flagon of cider. There is also a sticky box with two dates in it and a collection of those long, grey nuts that nobody ever eats. We are glad we have given up smoking, because the case of cigar-type Panatellas has been reduced to ashes. The Christmas cards, once so neat, have been hit by elbows and draughts and there are gaps on the mantelpiece that somehow put me in mind of a Hallowe'en mask. The heavy roller appears to have been used upon the careful arrangement of holly and pine. The Christmas tree is shedding determinedly. This is the sombre aftermath.

A clue to how sombre the aftermath would be was given to us on the very day after Boxing Day. The dog barked in the careful way that she reserves for the postman. I went to the back door. A uniformed official of the Electricity Board handed me my quarterly account. Until now we have not dared look at it, but on this evening of reckoning it can almost be tolerated when compared with the half year's rates (now due) — and with the gas bill, the coal bill and half a dozen similar little pretties leering in the background. We are also very much aware that it will not be long before we bow before the reckonings for those massive last-minute Christmas follies . . .

It is one of life's sharp ignominies that in the dark days of January and February, when every kind of soothing comfort is necessary as a reminder that April will one day be coming, the most rigorous economy campaign of the year becomes inevitable. If ever there was a fine example of Crime and Punishment, this is it. Yet I am certain of this: if we survive the existing crises without the intervention of the Trustee in Bankruptcy, by next December — or even late November — we'll be in there struggling again, accumulating the psychedelic trophies of a commercial Christmas, counting the days till it happens.